GLORIOUS BRITAIN

ILLUSTRATED WITH PHOTOGRAPHS FROM
THE FRANCIS FRITH COLLECTION

WITH QUOTATIONS FROM WRITERS AND TRAVELLERS FROM THE PAST

RICHMOND, THE CASTLE AND BRIDGE 1893   *32275t*

GLORIOUS BRITAIN

ILLUSTRATED WITH PHOTOGRAPHS FROM

THE FRANCIS FRITH COLLECTION

WITH QUOTATIONS FROM WRITERS AND TRAVELLERS FROM THE PAST

Compiled and edited by Terence Sackett

First published in the United Kingdom in 2005 by The Francis Frith Collection

Hardback Edition Published in 2005 ISBN 1-84589-115-5

British Library Cataloguing in Publication Data

Glorious Britain
Compiled and edited by Terence Sackett

The Francis Frith Collection
Frith's Barn, Teffont,
Salisbury, Wiltshire SP3 5QP
Tel: +44 (0) 1722 716 376
Email: info@francisfrith.co.uk
www.francisfrith.co.uk

Printed in Singapore by Imago

Front Cover: Windsor, Castle Hill 1906 *53719t*

CONTENTS

FRANCIS FRITH
VICTORIAN PIONEER

FRANCIS FRITH, founder of the world-famous photographic archive, was a complex and multi-talented man. A devout Quaker and a highly successful Victorian businessman, he was philosophical by nature and pioneering in outlook.

By 1855 he had already established a wholesale grocery business in Liverpool, and sold it for the astonishing sum of £200,000, which is the equivalent today of over £15,000,000. Now a very rich man, he was able to indulge his passion for travel. As a child he had pored over travel books written by early explorers, and his fancy and imagination had been stirred by family holidays to the sublime mountain regions of Wales and Scotland. 'What lands of spirit-stirring and enriching scenes and places!' he had written. He was to return to these scenes of grandeur in later years to 'recapture the thousands of vivid and tender memories', but with a different purpose. Now in his thirties, and captivated by the new science of photography, Frith set out on a series of pioneering journeys up the Nile and to the Near East that occupied him from 1856 until 1860.

INTRIGUE AND EXPLORATION

These far-flung journeys were packed with intrigue and adventure. In his life story, written when he was sixty-three, Frith tells of being held captive by bandits, and of fighting 'an awful midnight battle to the very point of surrender with a deadly pack of hungry, wild dogs'. Wearing flowing Arab costume, Frith arrived at Akaba by camel sixty years before Lawrence of Arabia, where he encountered 'desert princes and rival sheikhs, blazing with jewel-hilted swords'.

He was the first photographer to venture beyond the sixth cataract of the Nile. Africa was still the mysterious 'Dark Continent', and Stanley and Livingstone's historic meeting was a decade into the future. The conditions for picture taking confound belief. He laboured for hours in his wicker dark-room in the sweltering heat of the desert, while the volatile chemicals fizzed dangerously in their trays. Back in London he exhibited his photographs and was 'rapturously cheered' by members of the Royal Society. His reputation as a photographer was made overnight.

VENTURE OF A LIFE-TIME

Characteristically, Frith quickly spotted the opportunity to create a new business as a specialist publisher of photographs. He lived in an era of immense and sometimes violent change. For the poor in the early part of Victoria's reign work was exhausting and the hours long, and people had precious little free time to enjoy themselves. Most had no transport other than a cart or gig at their disposal, and rarely travelled far beyond the boundaries of their own town or village. However, by the 1870s the railways had threaded their way across the country, and Bank Holidays and half-day Saturdays had been made obligatory by Act of Parliament. All of a sudden the working man and his family were able to enjoy days out and see a little more of the world.

With typical business acumen, Francis Frith foresaw that these new tourists would enjoy having souvenirs to commemorate their days out. In 1860 he married Mary Ann Rosling and set out on a new career: his aim was to photograph every city, town and village in Britain. For the next thirty years he travelled the country by train and by pony and trap, producing fine photographs of seaside resorts and beauty spots that were keenly bought by millions of Victorians. These prints were painstakingly pasted into family albums and pored over during the dark nights of winter, rekindling memories of summer excursions.

THE RISE OF FRITH & CO

Frith's studio was soon supplying retail shops all over the country. To meet the demand he gathered about him a small team of photographers, and published the work of independent artist-photographers of the calibre of Roger Fenton and Francis Bedford. In order to gain some understanding of the scale of Frith's business one only has to look at the catalogue issued by Frith & Co in 1886: it runs to some 670 pages, listing not only many thousands of views of the British Isles but also many photographs of most European countries, and China, Japan, the USA and Canada. By 1890 Frith had created the greatest specialist photographic publishing company in the world, with over 2,000 sales outlets - more than the combined number that Boots and WH Smith have today!

POSTCARD BONANZA

The ever-popular holiday postcard we know today took many years to develop. The Post Office issued the first plain cards in 1870 , with a pre-printed stamp on one face. In 1894 they allowed other publishers' cards to be sent through the mail with an attached adhesive halfpenny stamp. Demand grew rapidly, and in 1895 a new size of postcard was permitted called the court card, but there was little room for illustration. In 1899, a year after Frith's death, a new card measuring 5.5 x 3.5 inches became the standard format, but it was not until 1902 that the divided back came into being, so that the address and message

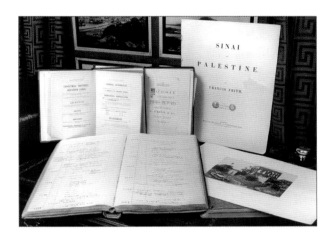

could be on one face and a full-size illustration on the other. Frith & Co were in the vanguard of postcard development: Frith's sons Eustace and Cyril continued their father's monumental task, expanding the number of views offered to the public and recording more and more places in Britain.

Francis Frith had died in 1898 at his villa in Cannes, his great project still growing. The archive he created continued in business for another seventy years. By 1970 it contained over a third of a million pictures showing 7,000 British towns and villages.

FRANCIS FRITH'S LEGACY

Frith's legacy to us today is of immense significance and value, for the magnificent archive of evocative photographs he created provides a unique record of change in the cities, towns and villages throughout Britain over a century and more. Frith and his fellow studio photographers revisited locations many times down the years to update their views, compiling for us an enthralling and colourful pageant of British life and character.

We are fortunate that Frith was dedicated to recording the minutiae of everyday life. For it is this sheer wealth of visual data, the painstaking chronicle of changes in dress, transport, street layouts, buildings, housing and landscape that captivates us so much today. His images offer us a powerful link with the past and with the lives of our ancestors.

THE VALUE OF THE ARCHIVE TODAY

Historians consider The Francis Frith Collection to be of prime national importance. It is the only archive of its kind remaining in private ownership. The archive's future is both bright and exciting. Francis Frith, with his unshakeable belief in making photographs available to the greatest number of people, would undoubtedly approve of the computer technology that allows his work to be rapidly transmitted to people all over by way of the internet. His photographs depicting our shared past are now bringing pleasure and enlightenment to millions around the world a century and more after his death.

INTRODUCTION

TWO hundred years ago, travelling through Britain would have been a true adventure. Walking or riding on horseback between north and south, east and west, or clattering along in a draughty, uncomfortable coach between the remote regions of Wales or Scotland and London would have been a daunting and difficult business. A journey of a hundred miles could take days, and simply reaching your destination without incident was a formidable achievement.

Because our towns and cities were so far distant from each other, each developed and expressed its own unique character. A journey of fifty miles really could take a traveller into foreign country – unlike today, when so many of us complain that everywhere we go is identical, no matter how far the distance.

The writers in this book reflect this extraordinary diversity of character. Their accounts recapture for us long-forgotten worlds, and they describe their experiences with style, considerable wit and deep feeling. Contemporary guidebooks, too, are quoted, and they enthuse in a florid style that writers on tourism today rarely copy or emulate.

There are surprises: it is difficult to believe, but William Cobbett detested Cheltenham. The American Henry James often casts unexpected but revealing light on places we may take for granted – for instance, beloved gems such as Westminster Abbey. However, most of the quotations express surprise and wonder at the sheer beauty of the scenes and sights they describe – Wilkie Collins at Tintagel, Carlyle at Stonehenge, Kilvert at Lynmouth, De Quincey on his first visit to Wordsworth's Dove Cottage, and Coleridge in Edinburgh. There is humour too – read Jerome K Jerome adrift on the crowded Thames during a hot summer weekend, and Thackeray on his disappointment at seeing the Giant's Causeway.

The superb photographs from The Francis Frith Collection, arranged region by region, are rich in detail, and will bring you a fascinating portrait of Britain as it was in years gone by. The quotations from writers, poets and travellers down the ages will enhance your enjoyment, and offer added insights into the extreme diversity of Britain's extraordinary history and heritage.

PLYMOUTH HOE

Devon

DRAKE'S ghost haunts Plymouth Hoe. It is difficult to cross this wide, breezy promenade without thinking of him. Sailor, circumnavigator, mayor, MP, bowls player, scourge of the Spanish – he crammed a lot into his 51 years. He sailed from Plymouth to 'singe the King of Spain's beard' at Cadiz in 1587, and returned to face his sternest test in 1588 – the Spanish Armada. His apparent bravado as the Armada was sighted in the English Channel – 'We have time to finish the game, and beat the Spaniards afterwards' – was dictated by the mundane fact that the tide was against him, so he could not have sailed just then anyway. However, the gesture was typical of the man, and cemented his place in history.

The Hoe that Drake knew was a very different place from the one we know today. The same limestone ridge endures, of course, from which the name is derived – 'hoe' comes from the Saxon for 'high place'. But long ago the Hoe was mostly devoid of buildings, and cattle and sheep grazed on the grass slopes, into which two enormous white figures were cut. These were Gogmagog and Corineus, two giants who legend said had fought on the Hoe. Their origin is unclear, but they remained there until 1671.

Left:
PLYMOUTH,
THE BARBICAN 1890
22474t

Right:
PLYMOUTH,
THE HOE 1904
52403

Below left:
PLYMOUTH,
DRAKE'S STATUE
1930 *83293*

We have time to finish the game, and beat the Spaniards afterwards … SIR FRANCIS DRAKE

GREAT DRAKE

SIR DRAKE, whome well the world's ends knewe
   Which thou didst compasse rounde:
And whome both poles of Heaven ons saw,
   Which North and South do bound :
The starrs above will make thee known,
   If men here silent were:
The Sunn himself cannot forgett
   His fellow Traveller.

Great Drake, whose shippe aboute the world's wide wast
   In three years did a golden girdle cast.
Who with fresh streames refresht this Towne that first,
   Though kist with waters, yet did pire for thirst.
Who both a Pilott and a Magistrate
   Steer'd in his turne the Shippe of Plymouth's state;
This little table shews his face whose worth
   The world's wide table hardly can sett forth.

ANON

CLOVELLY
North Devon

THE only safe anchorage on the inhospitable, craggy coastline between Appledore and Boscastle, Clovelly lived precariously for centuries from the herring fishery. However, Charles Kingsley's use of the village as a location in 'Westward Ho!' alerted the new breed of holidaymaker to the charm of its steep, cobbled streets; by 1890 there were three hotels.

The steepness of the High Street (known as Up-a-Long and Down-a-Long) meant that the mail had to be delivered by donkeys. Herring, coal and lime also came up the hill from the harbour. The donkeys were even used to collect the refuse.

Clovelly's remarkable state of preservation is due to the philanthropic nature of the Hamlyn family, who acquired the manor in 1740. Christine Hamlyn took charge of things in 1886 and founded the Clovelly Estate Company, which runs the village to this day.

Top:
CLOVELLY,
THE HARBOUR 1910
61014

Right:
CLOVELLY,
THE PIER AND
FISHING BOATS
C1871   *5916*

Opposite:
CLOVELLY,
MAIN STREET 1894
33490t

We slipped into the little pier, from whence the red-sailed herring boats were swarming forth like bees out of a hive ...

ARRIVING AT CLOVELLY

THE rock clefts grew sharper and sharper before us. The soft masses of the lofty bank of wooded cliff rose higher and higher. The white houses of Clovelly, piled stair above stair up the rocks, gleamed more and more brightly out of the green round bosoms of the forest. As we shut in headland after headland, one tall conical rock after another darkened with its black pyramid the bright orb of the setting sun. Soon we began to hear the soft murmur of the snowy surf line; then the merry voices of the children along the shore; and running straight for the cliff-foot, we slipped into the little pier, from whence the red-sailed herring boats were swarming forth like bees out of a hive, full of gay handsome faces, and all the busy blue-jacketed life of seaport towns, to their night's fishing in the bay.

CHARLES KINGSLEY, 'PROSE IDYLLS' 1849

9

Left:
LYNMOUTH AND
COUNTISBURY HILL
1929 *82198*

Right:
LYNMOUTH,
THE HARBOUR 1899
43095

Below right:
LYNTON,
THE VALLEY OF THE
ROCKS HOTEL 1907
59372

LYNMOUTH, set on the rocky north coast of Devon, was 'discovered' in 1812 by the poet Percy Bysshe Shelley, who stayed here with Harriet Westbrook, his first wife. They spent nine weeks here and spread word of its beauty to other poets such as Wordsworth, Coleridge and Southey, who described Lynmouth as 'the finest spot … that I ever saw'.

Lynton perches at the top of a 1-in-4 hill that leads down to Lynmouth. Visitors can also reach Lynmouth by way of a spectacular cliff railway that descends a sheer cliff of 500 feet. Close by Lynton is the Valley of the Rocks, a 'convulsion of Nature', popular with Victorian artists, and other seekers after the sublime and picturesque. Huge rocks lean precariously, the stacks forming fantastic shapes that worked on the poetic fancy of early visitors.

The scene which was clothed in darkness as we came in last night now lay suddenly revealed in the full splendour of the brilliant morning light, glowing with all its superb colouring …   FRANCIS KILVERT

SUNDAY, 14 SEPTEMBER 1873

I GOT up at 6 o'clock as the sun was rising behind the Tors. The house was silent and no one seemed to be about … It was one of the loveliest mornings that ever dawned upon this world …

The clear pure crisp air of the early morning blew fresh and exhilarating as the breeze came sweet from the sea. No one was astir, everything was silent, and I seemed to have the beautiful world to myself. The only sound that broke the stillness was the roaring of the Lyn far below. The scene which was clothed in darkness as we came in last night now lay suddenly revealed in the full splendour of the brilliant morning light, glowing with all its superb colouring, the red cliffs of the mighty Tors, the purple heather slopes and the rich brown wilderness of rusting fern, the snowy foam fringe chafing the feet of the cliffs, and the soft blue playing into green in the shoaling water of the bay where the morning was spread upon the sea.

In the quiet early sunny morning it seemed to me as if that place must be one of the loveliest nooks in the Paradise of this world.

FRANCIS KILVERT (1840–1879), DIARIES

SUCH is the scene – strange compound of fiction and truth, of the typical and the real – which legends teach us to imagine in the Tintagel Castle of thirteen centuries ago! … The grass grows high and luxuriant, where the rushes were strewn over the floor of Arthur's banqueting hall. Sheep are cropping the fresh pasture, within the walls which once echoed to the sweetest songs, or rang to the clash of the stoutest swords of ancient England! About the fortess, nothing remains unchanged, but … the sea that rolls and dashes, as at first, against its foundation rocks; and the wild Cornish country outspread on either side of it, as desolately and as magnificently as ever.

WILKIE COLLINS, 'RAMBLES BEYOND RAILWAYS', 1849

TINTAGEL

Cornwall

FABLED Tintagel is the legendary birthplace of King Arthur. The cliffs and castle are sublime, with plunging chasms and precipices, and rough fragments of wall, bastion and gateway bound by china clay mortar. Here (33595a), the ragged clouds and the sheep shining in the stormy light combine to create a fanciful, romantic scene.

Situated almost a mile inland from the castle, Tintagel village has a single plain street, a confusion of antique slate buildings and tawdry modern bungalows and shops. On the left of 33602, the lumpy roofs of the 14th-century Old Post Office plunge and pitch, the stout chimneys poking at the sky. The building fell into disrepair in the early part of the 20th century, but has now been completely restored by the National Trust.

Sheep are cropping the fresh pasture, within the walls which once echoed to the sweetest songs, or rang to the clash of the stoutest swords of ancient England!

WILKIE COLLINS

Opposite:
TINTAGEL, KING
ARTHUR'S CASTLE
1936 *87592*

Above left:
TINTAGEL, THE
VILLAGE 1894 *33602*

Below left:
TINTAGEL, KING
ARTHUR'S CASTLE
1894 *33595a*

Below right:
TINTAGEL 1895
36987

13

HARDY COUNTRY

Dorset

THOMAS Hardy was born in this picturesque cottage (right, 83400), a few miles to the west of Dorchester, in 1840. It was built by his grandfather, and Hardy wrote his first three novels whilst living here.

The county town of Dorchester is for ever Casterbridge, capital of the Wessex of Hardy's marvellous novels. There is probably no better way of exploring its streets than with a copy of 'The Mayor of Casterbridge', following in the steps of Hardy's tragic hero Michael Henchard. Such a stroll will reveal many of Dorchester's odd and delightful corners. This tour should be supplemented by a visit to the local museum, where Hardy's study has been meticulously recreated.

Hardy, who was a qualified architect, designed the house he was to live in for the next 53 years. Max Gate, (below, 83402), is very different from his rural childhood home. In this rather plain house he lived with his first wife Emma Gifford, who died in 1912. In 1914 he married Florence Dugdale, and they entertained many of the literary figures of the day, including T E Lawrence and J M Barrie. Hardy died at Max Gate on 11 January 1928.

Above:
HIGHER
BOCKHAMPTON,
HARDY'S
BIRTHPLACE 1930
83400

Left:
DORCHESTER,
MAX GATE 1930
83402

Right:
DORCHESTER,
THE THOMAS HARDY
MEMORIAL C1965
D44101

Opposite:
DORCHESTER,
THE KINGS ARMS
HOTEL 1913 *65626t*

LULWORTH COVE

AT LAST he [Troy] reached the summit, and a wide and novel prospect burst upon him with an effect almost like that of the Pacific on Balboa's gaze. The broad steely sea, marked only by faint lines, which had a semblance of being etched thereon to a degree not deep enough to disturb its general evenness, stretched the whole width of his front and round to the right, where, near the town and port of Budmouth [Weymouth], the sun bristled down upon it, and banished all colour, to substitute in its place a clear oily polish. Nothing moved in sky, land, or sea, except a frill of milk-white foam along the nearer angles of the shore, shreds of which licked the contiguous stones like tongues.

He descended and came to a small basin of sea enclosed by the cliffs [Lulworth Cove]. Troy's nature freshened within him; he thought he would rest and bathe here before going further. He undressed and plunged in. Inside the cove the water was uninteresting to a swimmer, being smooth as a pond, and to get a little of the ocean swell Troy presently swam between the two projecting spurs of rock which formed the Pillars of Hercules to this miniature Mediterranean. Unfortunately for Troy a current unknown to him existed outside, which, unimportant to craft of any burden, was awkward for a swimmer who might be taken in it unawares. Troy found himself carried to the left and then round in a swoop out to sea.

THOMAS HARDY (1840–1928)
'FAR FROM THE MADDING CROWD'

Opposite:
LULWORTH COVE 1894
34569

Above:
MELBURY OSMOND
(HARDY'S GREAT
HINTOCK), THE
VILLAGE AND BRIDGE
FARM C1955 *M216002*

Right:
WOOL, WOOLBRIDGE
MANOR 1904 *52731*
Here Angel Clare and Tess
spent their honeymoon.

LYME REGIS
Dorset

THERE *was too much wind to make the high part of the new Cobb pleasant for the ladies, and they agreed to get down the steps to the lower, and all were contented to pass quietly and carefully down the steep flight, excepting Louisa; she must be jumped down them by Captain Wentworth … He advised her against it, thought the jar too great; but no, he reasoned and talked in vain; she smiled and said, 'I am determined I will:' he put out his hands; she was too precipitate by half a second, she fell on the pavement on the lower Cobb, and was taken up lifeless!*

JANE AUSTEN (1775–1817), 'PERSUASION'

LYME Regis. Very fine. Tennyson up first and at my door. He has been on the Cobb, and eats a hearty breakfast. We go down to the Cobb, enjoying the sea, the breeze, the coast-view of Portland, etc, and while we sit on the wall I read to him, out of 'Persuasion'.

WILLIAM ALLINGHAM
SUNDAY, 26 AUGUST 1867

THE harbour of this little town at the south-western extremity of the county is renowned for its curious curved stone breakwater and quay, the Cobb, which was first erected in the reign of Edward I, and has been refurbished and maintained over successive eras. Lyme Regis is the setting of Jane Austen's novel 'Persuasion' and John Fowles's 'The French Lieutenant's Woman'.

Bridge Street (61625, below) is still one of the narrowest main roads in Dorset. The Victorians flocked to Lyme in search of fossils. The Fossil Depot shown here was the first permanent fossil shop in Lyme. It was demolished when Bridge Street was widened in 1913.

The fine study of the Granny's Teeth steps on the Cobb (65040, right) shows the setting of the incident in Jane Austen's novel 'Persuasion' where Louisa Musgrove falls off the wall. Jane Austen visited Lyme and adored the town and its setting. 'The young people were all wild to see Lyme', she wrote, as her characters approached the town.

Opposite:
LYME REGIS,
VICTORIA PIER 1912
65043

Left:
LYME REGIS, THE COBB
1912 *65040*

Below left:
LYME REGIS,
BRIDGE STREET 1909
61625

Below right:
LYME REGIS,
THE HARBOUR 1892
31308

19

IN SO far as beauty of structure is beauty of line and curve, balance and harmony of masses and dimensions, I have seldom relished it as deeply as on the grassy nave of some crumbling church, before lonely columns and empty windows where the wild flowers were a cornice and the sailing clouds a roof. The arts certainly hang together in what they do for us. These hoary relics of Glastonbury reminded me in their broken eloquence of one of the other great ruins of the world – the Last Supper of Leonardo. A beautiful shadow, in each case, is all that remains; but that shadow is the soul of the artist.

HENRY JAMES 1872

GLASTONBURY
Somerset

GLASTONBURY, with its mysterious and atmospheric tor, is still a place of legends. Besides connections with Arthur, there is a story that Joseph of Arimathea, in whose tomb Jesus was buried, came here as a trader and brought the Glastonbury Thorn. It is now thought that this legend was concocted around the 13th century by the monks of Glastonbury Abbey.

The most influential individual in the early development of the abbey was Dunstan, born nearby at Baltonsborough and abbot from 940 to 956. He extended the buildings and reformed the monks' lifestyle with the introduction of the rule of St Benedict.

In 1184 fire destroyed most of the building, and almost the whole complex had to be rebuilt. The date of rebuilding is usually given as 1186, although in reality it must have been spread over several years. The abbey, and its abbots, grew increasingly wealthy over the centuries, and Glastonbury was one of the main targets of Henry VIII's Dissolution of the Monasteries in the 1530s. Thereafter much of the stonework of the abandoned abbey was robbed for re-use elsewhere. In 1907 the site was bought on behalf of the Church of England.

In 64486 we are looking from the north along the line of the walls. The Chapel of St Thomas the Martyr (better known as Thomas à Becket) is at the end, through an archway to the left.

These hoary relics of Glastonbury reminded me in their broken eloquence of one of the other great ruins of the world – the Last Supper of Leonardo.   HENRY JAMES

Opposite page:
GLASTONBURY
ABBEY,
ST JOSEPH'S
CHAPEL 1904
52051t

Left:
GLASTONBURY
ABBEY, TRANSEPT
ARCHES 1912
64486

SALISBURY

Wiltshire

I HAVE been walking round the cathedral … From the centre of all this, that glorious spire rises – the work of a slightly later hand – too huge, I believe, for the rest of the cathedral, its weight having split and crushed its supporters. Fit emblem of the result of curbing systems. The moment the tower escapes above the level of the roof, it bursts into the wildest luxuriance, retaining the general character of the building below, but disguising it in a thousand fantastic excrescences – like the mind of man, crushed by human systems, and then suddenly asserting its own will in some burst of extravagance.

CHARLES KINGSLEY (1819–1875)

Salisbury Cathedral, my dear Jonas, is an edifice replete with venerable associations, and strikingly suggestive of the loftiest emotions. CHARLES DICKENS, 'MARTIN CHUZZLEWIT'

IN a scene that has changed little in a hundred years, the tranquil surface of the River Avon gently reflects the majesty of Salisbury Cathedral and its magnificent 404ft spire, the highest in England. Charles Kingsley, author of 'The Water Babies', and a devout Christian cleric for the greater part of his life, clearly had mixed feelings about the impact of the spire – see his comments opposite. Perhaps he was simply overcome by its raw power. The famous water meadows on the right of the picture, painted by John Constable, still exist (below, 65306a): the fields on the left are now the Queen Elizabeth Gardens and open to the public. Within the short span of 40 years (1220–1260) the cathedral was built in one Gothic style, Early English.

The High Street Gate (sometimes called the North Gate), is still closed every evening, a practice that has continued since the 1300s when the wall surrounding the cathedral was completed, thus emphasising that the cathedral and town were separate entities. The gatehouse housed a night porter and a small gaol.

In the view of the High Street (top right, 80922), the High Street Gate can be seen in the distance.

Opposite:
SALISBURY,
THE CATHEDRAL FROM THE RIVER
1887 *19730p*

Left:
SALISBURY,
THE CATHEDRAL FROM THE
MEADOWS 1831, JOHN CONSTABLE
65306a

Right:
SALISBURY,
HIGH STREET GATE 1894 *34872*

Above right:
SALISBURY, HIGH STREET 1928
80922t

STONEHENGE

Wiltshire

STONEHENGE is the most well-known stone circle in the world, and the view shown right (80950) is possibly one of the most photographed. It shows the Hele stone between the middle upright. The monument is perennially popular with modern-day Druids who congregate here to celebrate the summer solstice, when the sun is said to rise directly above the Hele stone on the longest day of the year, 21 June. However, the sun does not actually rise directly above it and never did, even 4,000 years ago.

As we look southwards from the Hele stone (19796) through the middle arch, we can see the tallest stone of the inner horseshoe of trilithons. The oldest tenon joint in Britain can be seen, laboriously hammered out with football-shaped flint hammers. The lintel that capped this stone contained the mortise to hold it in place. This was a remarkable achievement for a stone erected some 4,000 years ago.

In the 19th century, visitors could hire hammers from the blacksmith at Amesbury to chip off fragments of the stones to keep as souvenirs!

That huge mass of dark, meaningless, gigantic dislocated stones; of which no creature will ever tell us the meaning ... THOMAS CARLYLE

Above: STONEHENGE 1928   *80950*   *Opposite:* STONEHENGE 1887   *19796*

IN THE grey windy evening [we] set forth to walk towards Stonehenge over the bare upland; found it, saw it: a wild mournful altogether enigmatic and bewildering sight; dreadfully cold too (in my thin coat), and after about two hours came our ways home again to Amesbury, an enchanted-looking village, very appropriate to the neighbourhood. Stonehenge and the uplands far and wide were utterly solitary; a vast, green, wavy tract of sheep-pasture, all studded with (what they call 'barrows') the tombs of extinct nations, and that huge mass of dark, meaningless, gigantic dislocated stones; of which no creature will ever tell us the meaning, except that it is the extinct temple of an extinct people seemingly sunk very deep in error and the prey now of Pedants and doleful creatures whose whole element seems one of emptiness and error! The grim windy evening, spent amid those grim remains, in a mood such as mine, will probably long continue memorable to me. And that hitherto seems all the conquest I am like to get from it.

THOMAS CARLYLE JULY 1848

THE wind, playing upon the edifice, produced a booming tune, like the note of some gigantic one-stringed harp. No other sound came from it, and lifting his hand and advancing a step or two, Clare felt the vertical surface of the structure. It seemed to be of solid stone, without joint or moulding. Carrying his fingers onward he found that what he had come in contact with was a colossal rectangular pillar; by stretching out his left hand he could feel a similar one adjoining. At an indefinite height overhead something made the black sky blacker, which had the semblance of a vast architrave uniting the pillars horizontally. They carefully entered beneath and between; the surfaces echoed their soft rustle; but they seemed to be still out of doors. The place was roofless. Tess drew her breath fearfully …

THOMAS HARDY, TESS OF THE D'URBEVILLES

THE WHITE CHALK HORSES
Wiltshire

THE white horses of the chalk downland in southern England are among the best-known features of the countryside. Other large-scale hillside figures cut into the turf (including giants, birds, crosses, badges and others) can be found all over Britain. This form of turf cutting is a very old and widespread art, albeit a rather obscure one, but it does seem to be a peculiarly English practice.

The Wessex region, with its abundance of chalk downlands, possesses most of the examples that have survived. Almost all of the horses were cut in the late 18th century, and a few in the 19th century. The reasons for such laborious work vary greatly, from the whim of the landowner to historical or religious significance, but the origins and purpose of the few examples from prehistoric times are still not known.

It was in 1804 that local schoolboys from Marlborough cut a horse into the chalk landscape. Meandering along its quiet way close by is the famous chalk river, the Kennet.

The present horse just outside Westbury dates from 1778 and was the first of several figures cut in the chalk downs of Wiltshire during the next half-century. Immediately above it is the outline of Bratton Camp, an Iron Age fortification.

BALLAD OF THE SCOURING OF THE WHITE HORSE

The owld White Horse wants zettin to rights
And the Squire hev promised good cheer,
Zo we'll gee un a scrape to kip un in zhape,
And a'll last for many a year.

A was made a lang lang time ago
Wi a good dale o' labour and pains,
By King Alfred the Great when he spiled their consate
And caddled they wosbirds the Danes.

The Bleawin Stwun in days gone by
Wur King Alfred's bugle harn,
And the tharning tree you may plainly zee
As is called King Alfred's tharn.

There'll be backsword play, and climmin the powl,
And a race for a peg and a cheese,
And us thenks as hisn's a dummel zowl
As dwont care for zich spwoorts as theze!

ANON

26

I may venture to hold a small wager, that should the horse scape a scouring but two seven years more his dapple would become a green one, which would be a still greater rarity for all true lovers of antiquity.

Dr Francis Wise 1738

Opposite below:
Westbury, The White Horse 1900
45365

Opposite above:
Marlborough, White Horse Hill
1901 *47767*

Above:
Uffington, The White Horse c1960
U24025

BY FAR the most important and best-known white horse lies on the Berkshire Downs at Uffington, close to several ancient earthworks and burial mounds, overlooking an area which has been known as the Vale of the White Horse for more than 1,000 years. To many people it is the most beautiful of all the hill figures in this country; it is certainly very old and mysterious. It is larger than all the subsequent horses at 365 feet in length; it is also quite different in appearance, facing right and apparently galloping. Its body is thin, almost stylised, with a bird-like head.

The ancient tradition of scouring the White Horse at Uffington was first mentioned by Thomas Baskerville in 1677. Yet the horse is centuries older, and the cleaning away of weeds and other debris to sharpen the outline has probably been going on since Norman times. The scouring was an occasion for jollity – there was always a fair with booths and stalls offering gingerbread, ribbons, and other trifles. Musicians and acrobats entertained the crowds. A song was written for the occasion, which is printed opposite.

Sᴜɴᴅᴀʏ 2 Jᴜɴᴇ 1799. *What must I tell you of Edward [Austen]? Truth or falsehood? I will try the former, and you may chuse for yourself another time. He was better yesterday than he had been for two or three days before, about as well as he was at Steventon. He drinks at the Hetling pump, is to bathe tomorrow, and try electricity on Tuesday; he proposed the latter himself to Dr Fellowes, who made no objection to it, but I fancy we are all unanimous in expecting no advantage from it …*

JANE AUSTEN (Eᴅᴡᴀʀᴅ ᴡᴀs sᴜꜰꜰᴇʀɪɴɢ ꜰʀᴏᴍ ɢᴏᴜᴛ)

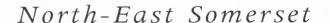

North-East Somerset

THE Roman town of Aquae Sulis had as its focus the hot spring-fed baths, where citizens of the Roman Empire flocked for rheumatic cures. The baths of the Romans were indeed sumptuous, and the remains, seen opposite (25135) before the 19th-century restoration, give the viewer some idea of their scale and fine architectural quality. In 1897 the architect John Brydon added dignified colonnades around the baths with balustrades and statues. Ever since, visitors have been heard to comment on the remarkable survival of so much original Roman work!

The panoramic view (left, 82323) was taken from the roof of Bath's old abbey, and looks north along the High Street with the domed Georgian guildhall on the right. Beyond is the quirky 1830s parish church of St Nicholas, now with the ultra-modern Podium shopping centre to its right.

THE first view of Bath in fine weather does not answer my expectations; I think I see more distinctly thro' rain. The sun was behind everything, and the appearance of the place from the top of Kingsdown was all vapour, shadow, smoke, and confusion ...

JANE AUSTEN

Opposite:
BATH, THE ROMAN
BATHS 1890 *25135*

Above:
BATH, THE VIEW
FROM THE ABBEY
1929 *82323*

Right:
BATH, THE ABBEY
AND THE PUMP ROOM
1929 *82332*

Then the streets, when you go into them, are as handsome and gay as London, gayer and handsomer because cleaner …

IF EVER you live in England you must live here at Bath. It really is a splendid city in a lovely, even a noble, country. Did you ever see it? … The streets, when you go into them, are as handsome and gay as London, gayer and handsomer because cleaner and in a cleaner atmosphere; and if you want the country you get into it (and a very fine country) on all sides and directly. Then there is such choice of houses, cheap as well as dear, of all sizes, with good markets, railways etc. I am not sure I shall not come here for part of the Winter. It is a place you would like, I am sure.

EDWARD FITZGERALD 1854

Left: BATH, ST MICHAEL'S CHURCH 1904   53000t

Above: BATH, QUEEN SQUARE 1901   46474

Opposite: BATH, THE PARAGON 1911   63684

IN THE 18th century, the city was effectively rebuilt, replanned and expanded, as wealthy visitors flocked to take the waters, to gamble, to attend assemblies and generally enjoy themselves during the Bath season. Beau Nash presided over the fashionable throng, while John Wood the elder provided the architectural genius to turn a provincial city into a 'new Rome'. He and his son were responsible for Bath's glories, including the Royal Crescent, Queen Square, and the North and South Parades. Here we see the Paragon, a superb terrace of 21 houses set between two roads on steeply differing levels, their stables and vaults fronting Walcot Street below.

A navigable estuary, a deep sea, a sheltered shore – all on a lovely island; what more could be desired? … They [East and West Cowes] present the most charming view imaginable, terrace upon terrace rising in masses of foliage, and rendering it a matter of some difficulty for the visitor to make up his mind on which side of the estuary he would like to land.

VICTORIAN GUIDEBOOK

COWES
Isle of Wight

WEST Cowes and East Cowes are situated on the west and east banks of the River Medina, and are famous throughout the world as a centre for yachting and as the home port of the Royal Yacht Squadron. Many visitors gain their first impressions of the Isle of Wight as they land by ferry from Southampton.

Cowes harbour is a fine natural anchorage which has been appreciated by sailors for centuries. The early local historian Sir John Oglander remarked that he saw some 300 ships riding at anchor there in 1620.

Cowes has always been more popular as a touring base than as a traditional seaside resort, though one rhymester tried to remedy the situation in 1760 when he wrote 'No more to foreign baths shall Britons roam, But plunge at Cowes, and find rich health at home!' Hotels and yacht chandlers line the seashore at Cowes. The town's importance as a centre for yachting, and the close proximity of Queen Victoria's home Osborne House, made Cowes most fashionable in the 19th century. A large number of hotels were built to cater for the increased number of tourists.

Cowes Week and the famous regatta first began in August 1826 under the flag of the Royal Yacht Club. Three days of intensive racing in the swift waters of the Solent were organised. So popular did the event become, that King George IV was encouraged to present a gold cup worth £100 to the winners to celebrate the occasion. Cowes Week runs for eight days, and is the longest-running regatta in the world.

Opposite:
COWES, THE REGATTA
1903 *50797b*

Above:
COWES, THE REGATTA
1903 *50797c*

Left:
COWES, THE ESPLANADE
1913 *66311*

PORTSMOUTH
Hampshire

RICHARD I was responsible for establishing a settlement on Portsea Island, and it was he who built the first dock at Portsmouth in the late 12th century. The Tudor kings Henry VII and VIII later constructed the first dry dock in the world here. A considerable amount of development took place here in the 17th and 18th centuries, including the building of naval establishments and factories. Most of the dockyard, where Nelson's flagship HMS 'Victory' has remained more or less intact since the battle of Trafalgar (below, 22754), also dates from around that time.

The photograph of the Hard (opposite, 22751), overlooking Portsmouth Harbour, shows at least three pubs - including the Victoria and Albert in the centre of the picture. The many waterfront drinking houses would have tempted Portsmouth's shifting population of sailors.

In August 1805, Napoleon instructed his admirals: 'Come into the Channel. Bring our united fleet and England is ours … six centuries of shame and insult will be avenged'. Nelson, however, saw matters differently. At the decisive battle of Trafalgar, he confronted the enemy fleet; the bloody battle in which he lost his life established England's naval supremacy, allowing the British Empire to be expanded and consolidated into the 20th century.

A DECISIVE stroke on their fleet would make half a peace, and, my dear Emma, if I can do that I shall as soon as possible ask to come home and get my rest – at least for the winter … What greater reward could the country bestow than to let me come to you and Horatia, and dear, dear Merton; and to come to you a victor would be a victory twice gained.

LORD NELSON, FROM A LETTER TO EMMA HAMILTON, 1805

Now I am satisfied. Thank God I have done my duty. God bless you, Hardy. LORD NELSON

Opposite:
PORTSMOUTH, THE HARD 1890 *22751*

Above:
PORTSMOUTH, THE HARBOUR 1892 *30004*

Left:
PORTSMOUTH, HMS 'VICTORY' 1890 *22754*

BRIGHTON

Sussex

IT IS a Piccadilly crowd by the sea – exactly the same style of people you meet in Piccadilly, but freer in dress, and particularly in hats. All fashionable Brighton parades the King's Road twice a day, morning and afternoon, always on the side of the shops. The route is up and down the King's Road as far as Preston Street, back again and up East Street. Riding and driving Brighton extends its Rotten Row sometimes to Third Avenue, Hove. These well-dressed and leading people never look at the sea. Watching by the gold-plate shop you will not observe a single glance in the direction of the sea, beautiful as it is, gleaming under the sunlight. They do not take the slightest interest in sea, or sun, or sky, or the fresh breeze calling white horses from the deep. Their pursuits are purely 'social', and neither ladies nor gentlemen ever go on the beach or lie where the surge comes to the feet. The beach is ignored; it is almost, perhaps quite vulgar; or rather it is entirely outside the pale. No one rows, very few sail; the sea is not 'the thing' in Brighton, which is the least nautical of seaside places. There is more talk of horses.

RICHARD JEFFERIES (1848–1887)

These well-dressed and leading people never look at the sea. Watching by the gold-plate shop you will not observe a single glance in the direction of the sea, beautiful as it is ...

RICHARD JEFFERIES

ONCE a modest fishing village, Brighton was transformed by the late 18th-century fashion for ozone and sea bathing. Only five hours from London, and endorsed by the Prince Regent, the settlement spread along the coast in stucco waves. The astonishing Brighton Pavilion (below right, 22244) started life as a farmhouse, then became a classical villa with a rotunda, before Beau Nash transformed it into a domed and minareted Indian-style palace fit for the Prince Regent.

Photograph 41890 (right) captures the tremendous bustle of Brighton. The beach is dotted with small sailing boats and lines of bathing machines. In the background is the Palace Pier, the chain pier's replacement, under construction.

The seafront was frequently battered by severe storms. The photograph below (B2085009) shows the damage caused by the 1896 storm to the West Pier, and to the partly-built Palace Pier.

The photograph on the opposite page (22345), shows the beach close by the West Pier. Here jugglers, clowns, musicians and conjurors would delight the crowds, and fishermen would arrange short sea trips in gaff-rigged yawls, like the one shown here.

Opposite:
BRIGHTON,
THE BEACH AND THE
WEST PIER 1889 *22345*

Below left:
BRIGHTON,
THE WEST PIER 1896
B2085009

Above right:
BRIGHTON,
THE BEACH 1898 *41890t*

Below right:
BRIGHTON,
THE PAVILION 1889
22244

THE castle stands out boldly on the opposite hill, while below lies the town and the rocky shore, which at low tide has the appearance of so many tongues, or fangs, running out into the sea. If the day be clear, too, one may see the French coast of Picardy – the spot from whence the Normans embarked.

VICTORIAN GUIDEBOOK

HASTINGS

Sussex

THE most momentous battle and best-known date in English history surely must be the battle of Hastings, 1066, when the Norman Duke William earned his title 'the Conqueror' by defeating the Saxon King Harold II. William landed at Pevensey, which at that time lay on the coast, not about a mile inland as it does today; he marched with his army to meet Harold at a suitable spot on a little hill just inland from Hastings. The town that has grown at the gates of the abbey William founded to mark his victory is known simply as Battle.

The remains of Hastings Castle (opposite, 22791), the first built by William the Conqueror, crown Hastings's West Hill, with superb views over the town and out to sea. Coastal erosion, culminating in a great storm in 1287, destroyed much of the castle fabric, seen in this picture as an ivy-covered ruin.

Until the 19th century, Hastings was a fishing port, and the tall weatherboarded net shops can still be found clustering on the foreshore below East Cliff. The town's sheltered situation – it sits in a snug hollow – encouraged visitors. Lord Byron and Charles Lamb have left records of their stay here, the latter characteristically describing his sojourn as 'a dreary penance'.

HIC·ODO EPS:BACVL

If I were a quiet old lady of modest income and nice habits – or even a quiet old gentleman of the same pattern – I should certainly go to Hastings. HENRY JAMES

Opposite:
HASTINGS, THE CASTLE
RUINS 1890 *22791*

Above:
HASTINGS, FROM EAST
CLIFF 1891 *29039*

Right:
HASTINGS, THE BEACH
1890 *25357*

BEACHY HEAD

Sussex

THIS infamous headland, at 536ft the highest cliff on the south coast, marks the point where the South Downs plunge into the English Channel. The red and white lighthouse at the foot of the cliffs is pictured during the time when the new work was being carried out; it was started in July 1899 and completed in 1902. The foundations of this 153ft-high tower were sunk 18 feet into the chalk, and about 3,600 tons of Cornish granite were used to build it. The light is visible for 16 miles.

Opposite:
BEACHY HEAD
1893   *50417*

Above:
BEACHY HEAD,
THE DOWNS
1912   *64983*

ANOTHER climb up from the sheep-path, and it is not far then to the terrible edge of that tremendous cliff which rises straighter than a ship's side out of the sea, six hundred feet above the detached rock below, where the limpets cling like rivet heads, and the sand rills run around it. But it is not possible to look down to it – the glance of necessity falls outwards, as a raindrop from the eaves is deflected by the wind, because it is the edge where the mould crumbles; the rootlets of the grass are exposed; the chalk is about to break away in flakes. You cannot lean over as over a parapet, lest such a flake should detach itself – lest a mere trifle should begin to fall, awakening a dread and dormant inclination to slide and finally plunge like it.   RICHARD JEFFERIES (1848–1887)

IT WAS late in the afternoon when I first entered the church; there had been a service in the choir, but that was well over, and I had the place to myself. The verger, who had some pushing-about of benches to attend to, turned me into the locked gates and left me to wander through the side aisles of the choir and into the great chapel beyond it … I made my way down into the crypt, which is a magnificent maze of low, dark arches and pillars, and groped about till I found the place where the frightened monks had first shuffled the inanimate victim of Moreville and Fitzurse out of the reach of further desecration. While I stood there a violent thunderstorm broke over the cathedral; great rumbling gusts and rain-drifts came sweeping through the open sides of the crypt and, mingling with the darkness which seemed to deepen and flash in corners and with the potent mouldy smell, made me feel as if I had descended into the very bowels of history.

HENRY JAMES 1877

Far left:
CANTERBURY,
THE CATHEDRAL,
NORTH GATE 1888
21358a

Opposite right:
CANTERBURY,
THE CATHEDRAL
CRYPT 1898 *40844*

CANTERBURY CATHEDRAL
Kent

THE historic city of Canterbury is dominated by its famous cathedral, and has since Saxon days been the spiritual capital of England. The cathedral was rebuilt in the 12th century, when it began to assume the form we see it in today. The nave was completed in 1405. The huge proportions and the nobility of the architecture are still breathtaking, almost 600 years later. It was in Canterbury Cathedral that Thomas à Becket was murdered in 1170, and the city has been a place of pilgrimage ever since. The crypt is the finest of its kind in the world. It dates from Norman times. The awesome majesty of the subterranean setting symbolises the ancient mysteries of the Christian tradition.

LONDON

The City

THIS quaint old house sits on a corner in Lincoln's Inn Fields (right, L130121). It has been claimed, probably erroneously, that it is the original of the Old Curiosity Shop made immortal by Dickens as the home of Little Nell. In the 1950s it became an exclusive antique shop but in Victorian times it was a rather dingy emporium owned by H Poole, a jobbing stationer.

Perched on the summit of Ludgate Hill at almost the highest point in the City, St Paul's Cathedral, Wren's masterpiece, is the pride of London (below, L130126). It is in the form of a cross, and built in the Corinthian style, and is surmounted by the giant dome which rises on arches over the centre. Many great men and women are buried here, including Wren himself, James Barrie, Sir Joshua Reynolds, and the painters Opie and Landseer. This panoramic vista of the City and St Paul's was probably taken from the southern tip of Southwark Bridge. In early days, Queenhithe on the north bank of the Thames was a significant port.

Left:
LONDON, PORTSMOUTH STREET, THE OLD CURIOSITY SHOP
c1875 *L130121p*

Below left:
LONDON, ST PAUL'S CATHEDRAL FROM ACROSS THE RIVER
1890 *L130126*

Opposite:
LONDON, THE BANK OF ENGLAND AND THE ROYAL EXCHANGE
c1910 *L130207*

LIKE the spokes of a wheel converging, streams of human life flow into this agitated pool of blue carts and yellow omnibuses, varnished carriages and brown vans … Men and women fill the interstices between the carriages and blacken the surface, till the vans almost float on human beings … This is the vortex and whirlpool, the centre of human life today on the earth. Here it seethes and whirls, not for an hour only, but for all present time, hour by hour, day by day, year by year.

RICHARD JEFFERIES (1848–1887), 'THE STORY OF MY HEART'

IN THE 1860s the economist Bagehot described the area of the City around the Bank of England and the Mansion House (right, L130207) as 'by far the greatest combination of economical power and economic delicacy that the world has ever seen'. With the coming of the railways and international currency dealings, the City began to prosper as it never had before, with small investors flocking to involve themselves in the heady world of stocks and shares.

THE scene in … Hyde Park, on fine afternoons, is most interesting and imposing. In the Drive are seen unbroken files of elegant equipages and high-bred horses in handsome trappings moving continually to and fro, presided over by sleek coachmen and powdered lackeys, and occupied by some of the most beautiful and exquisitely dressed women in the world. In the Row are numerous riders, who parade their spirited and glossy steeds before the admiring crowd sitting or walking at the sides.

KARL BAEDEKER, 'LONDON AND ITS ENVIRONS: A HANDBOOK FOR TRAVELLERS' 1900

THE West End has long been the most fashionable region of London. Simply having an address there was an advantage. Robert Southey said that his tailor lived at the West End of town, 'and consequently he is supposed to make my coat in a better style of fashion'.

Hyde Park (opposite, L130105) extends from Piccadilly westwards to Kensington Gardens. Its 360 acres of open green space were called by William Pitt 'the lung of London'. 'Here', writes Thomas Miller, 'the pride and beauty of England may be seen upon their own stage; and on a fine day in the season no other spot in the world can outrival in rich display and chaste grandeur the scene which is here presented'.

The view of Regent Street (below left, L130079) looks north towards Oxford Street. Nash's handsome terraces were spurned by London's affluent classes, for stucco was considered common. Some said that his glorious creation was compromised by poor building work, but all agreed that Nash conjured for this region of the West End a genteel and polished atmosphere that has considerably added to its prosperity down the years.

The handsome triple-arched gateway at Hyde Park Corner (above left, L130151), with its classical screen and groups of Ionic columns, was intended originally to create a noble approach to the park from Buckingham Palace. It was designed and built in 1828 by Decimus Burton. The omnibus on the right, heading for Pimlico, is advertising the famous furnishing and decorating emporium of Maples.

Opposite:
LONDON, HYDE PARK
1890 *L130105*

Aove left:
LONDON, HYDE PARK
CORNER C1908 *L130151*

Below left:
LONDON, REGENT STREET
C1890 *L130079*

LONDON
Westminster

THIS sublime abbey, scene of many coronations down the centuries, is probably the most famous of English religious buildings, and is considered the pinnacle of European Gothic. Henry II began the reshaping of Edward the Confessor's old church. Restyling continued until well into the 16th century. The abbey was embellished by its lofty twin towers in the early 1700s.

Behind the abbey (L130162p opposite) are Big Ben and the Houses of Parliament. The Westminster Column, an imposing monument of red granite designed by Gilbert Scott in memory of pupils of Westminster School who had fallen in the Crimea, was added to a site just outside the entrance in 1861. Four imposing lions crouch at its base.

Westminster's fine bridge is one of the most dazzling structures spanning London's river, and was constructed in 1862 at a cost of £250,000. With the waters at low tide as they are here, critics have suggested the bridge has an ungraceful lanky appearance. Its uniquely light construction was the cause of trepidation amongst Londoners, for passengers on horse-drawn buses felt an unnerving vibration under the wheels as they passed over.

Left:
LONDON, WESTMINSTER ABBEY, THE NAVE ALTAR c1965 *L1305262*

Right:
LONDON, WESTMINSTER ABBEY c1867 *L130142*

Opposite:
LONDON, WESTMINSTER BRIDGE 1890 *L130162p*

I WALKED down to Westminster Abbey on Good Friday afternoon – walked from Piccadilly across the Green Park and through that of St James. The parks were densely filled with the populace – the elder people shuffling about the walks and the poor little smutty-faced children sprawling over the dark damp turf. When I reached the Abbey I found a dense group of people about the entrance, but I squeezed my way through them and succeeded in reaching the threshold. Beyond this it was impossible to advance, and I may add that it was not desirable. I put my nose into the church and promptly withdrew it. The crowd was terribly compact, and beneath the Gothic arches the odour was not that of incense. I gradually gave it up, with that very modified sense of disappointment that one feels in London at being crowded out of a place.

HENRY JAMES 1877

THE Palace of Westminster, the 'superb temple of legislation' in Victorian Gothic, was built to replace the old medieval palace which burned down in 1834. Covering nearly eight acres of ground, it was constructed to Sir Charles Barry's design, although its intricate ornament and detailing were conceived and wrought by that master of Victorian Gothic, Augustus Pugin.

The finest prospect of Barry's Palace of Westminster is to be enjoyed from the river, where the facade extends to a length of almost 1,000 feet. The strong vertical detailing was clearly intended to create the impression of a just and God-fearing Parliament aspiring to the heavenly virtues.

In 1848 a serious drainage problem was discovered inside the Parliament building. A main sewer, passing directly underneath, was discharging into the river under Westminster Bridge. The malodorous gas from this sewer was so dreadful that it extinguished the lamps of the investigating party. Many of the underground apartments were found to be little more than open cesspools.

The monumental clock tower (right, L130008), surmounted by a richly-decorated belfry and spire, known more popularly as Big Ben, was designed by E B Denison in 1858 after considerable technical difficulties. The great bell, weighing sixteen tons, was cast at Stockton-on-Tees. It is thought that the clock tower was named after Sir Benjamin Hall, the Commissioner of Works for the project.

Opposite: LONDON, THE HOUSES OF PARLIAMENT 1908 *L130149*

Above: LONDON, THE HOUSES OF PARLIAMENT, THE HOUSE OF LORDS 1886 *L130231*

Right: LONDON, PARLIAMENT SQUARE 1890 *L130008p*

LONDON

Queen Victoria's Diamond Jubilee

QUEEN VICTORIA lived from 1819 to 1901. Her reign spanned two generations. By 1850 her loyal subjects had borrowed their sovereign's name and were calling themselves 'Victorians'. The young and popular queen reigned over a land that ruled the world, and her subjects were proud of her and of their country's achievements and potential. Britain was in the midst of creating the world's first great industrial power and this process necessarily involved a period of upheaval and social change.

Inherent was a deep-ingrained instinct for nationalism which bonded the nation together in difficult and troublesome times. The Victorians were never slow in celebrating a civic occasion, and thronged the streets whenever a gesture of loyalty to queen and country was required. It is not surprising, therefore, that in 1897, when the time of the queen's Diamond Jubilee came around, that the whole of London flocked to honour her. They cheered the military and its colourful pageantry, and the endless procession of carriages containing dignitaries. 'Vanity Fair' pronounced on the day's proceedings: 'We are a great people and we realised it on Saturday as we never realised it before'.

Below (L130157) we see the royal coach heading out across the courtyard of Buckingham Palace bound for the Mall. A throng of carriages waits to join the procession across London. Queen Victoria wrote in her diary that it was 'a never-to-be-forgotten day ... No one ever, I believe, has met with such an ovation as was given to me ... Every face seemed to be filled with real joy'.

Above: QUEEN VICTORIA *F6505*

Right: LONDON, BUCKINGHAM PALACE 1897 *L130157*

Left: QUEEN VICTORIA'S SEAL C1900 *L130236*

Opposite: LONDON, WESTMINSTER BRIDGE 1897 *L130219*

The heat during the last hour was very great, and poor Lord Howe ... fainted and had a bad fall ...

WE *proceeded over London Bridge, where no spectators were allowed, only troops, and then along the Borough Road, where there is a very poor population, but just as enthusiastic and orderly as elsewhere. The decorations there were very pretty, consisting chiefly of festoons of flowers on either side of the street. Crossed the river again over Westminster Bridge, past the Houses of Parliament, through Whitehall, Parliament Street, which has been much enlarged, through the Horse Guards and down the Mall. The heat during the last hour was very great, and poor Lord Howe, who was riding as Gold Stick, fainted and had a bad fall, but was not seriously hurt.*

QUEEN VICTORIA, DIARY 1897

WE went up Constitution Hill and Piccadilly, and there were seats right along the former, where my own servants and personal attendants, and members of the other Royal Households, the Chelsea Pensioners, and the children of the Duke of York's and Greenwich schools had seats. St James's Street was beautifully decorated with festoons of flowers across the road and many loyal inscriptions. Trafalgar Square was very striking, and outside the National Gallery stands were erected for the House of Lords. The denseness of the crowds was immense ... As we neared St Paul's the procession was often stopped, and the crowds broke out into singing God Save the Queen ...

QUEEN VICTORIA, DIARY 1897

OPPOSITE (L130158) we see Queen Victoria smiling graciously at her subjects from beneath a parasol. The team of horses bend under the weight of shining brasses and decorative harness. Behind the coach stands a gathering of robed dignitaries of the church.

One of the great city institutions, possibly the Mansion House (above left, L130010), is hung with swags of flowers and garlands for the great occasion. The porch has a decorative pelmet embroidered with a message celebrating the 60 glorious years of the queen's reign. A crowd has gathered outside, anxious to catch a glimpse of their sovereign and to catch a few words of the ceremony.

Preparations for the Jubilee celebrations would have taken the people of London many weeks to arrange. Below right (L130145) we see decorations being erected in Park lane. Rickety ladders are leaning up against buildings as workmen hang swags and bunting.

Opposite: LONDON, DIAMOND JUBILEE DAY 1897 *L130158*

Above: LONDON, THE DIAMOND JUBILEE 1897 *L130010*

Right: LONDON, PARK LANE, DIAMOND JUBILEE DECORATIONS 1897 *L130145*

EPSOM is famous for two things: Epsom Salts, and the two great classic flat races run on the Downs south of the town, the Derby and the Oaks, both inaugurated in the late 18th century. The salts gave the town its first fame in the 17th century as a noted spa town, but the May race meeting still remains very popular and draws huge crowds. The view (left) shows the bookies doing a roaring trade.
The name of the race was decided after the Earl of Derby and Sir Charles Bunbury, a great racing enthusiast, flipped a coin. So begun the inaugural running of the 'Derby' won, incidentally, by Sir Charles Bunbury's horse Diomed.

Off they go! The photograph bottom left (E37001) probably shows the start of the 1882 Derby. It was won that year by the Duke of Westminster's Shotover.

The grandstand in 1928 (left, 81595) accommodated 20,000 people, compared with the 6,000 of the 1830 grandstand. An estimated 512,000 people watched the race that year.

Above:
EPSOM
RACECOURSE,
DERBY DAY 1928
81595p

Right:
EPSOM
RACECOURSE,
THE START OF
THE DERBY
C1882 E37001

Opposite:
EPSOM
RACECOURSE,
THE
GRANDSTAND
C1955 E37136

Stuffy always … in summer-time it would have been not a bad training for the Black Hole of Calcutta .

IN THE lower part of the Upper School are small chambers intended to be used as class-rooms. Look into one. It is a small, ill-lighted room, perhaps fifteen feet square, and far from lofty, occupied by four or five rows of benches. The doorway opens into a passage, or annexe, in which, just beyond the swing of the door, there is room for a small desk placed sideways, and a chair. In this cell, the only well-ventilated place in the room – and a wind-swept corner it must have been in winter – sat the master, looking out upon his class, which often consisted of some thirty boys. Stuffy always this den must have been, but in summer-time it would have been not a bad training for the Black Hole of Calcutta.

TOURIST GUIDE 1895

ETON COLLEGE
Berkshire

ETON COLLEGE was founded by Henry VI in 1440. It was originally intended that there would be ten priests, four clerks, six choristers and a school for 25 poor scholars. Almost immediately the number of scholars was raised to 70. Today there are well over 1,000. Until the mid-19th century only Classics had been taught at the college; at this time the curriculum was widened.

Eton College schoolboys, with their tailed coats, have been, and still are, an integral part of the daily life in the High Street. The long-tailed coats are still worn, but the top hat has gone.

Eton High Street was originally the main thoroughfare through Eton; before road improvements were made during the Victorian era, it was quite often a quagmire, especially in wet conditions. When the postal numbering of premises changed to having all odd numbers on one side of the road and even on the other, Eton did not change, and all the numbers run consecutively up one side and down the other. A number of the old buildings still exist. One in particular, the Cockpit, is older than the college, dating back to 1420. Cock fights used to be held at the back of the building, which was originally made up of three cottages.

Opposite:
ETON,
THE COLLEGE, BARNES
POOL 1914 *67007p*

Above:
ETON,
HIGH STREET 1906
56036a

Left:
ETON,
THE FOURTH OF JUNE
PROCESSION OF BOATS
1906 *53724*

ROYAL WINDSOR
Berkshire

… A view altogether different in character, though scarcely less beautiful, was offered to the gaze. It was formed by the town of Windsor, then not a third of its present size, but incomparably more picturesque in appearance, consisting almost entirely of a long straggling row of houses, chequered black and white, with tall gables, and projecting storeys skirting the west and south sides of the castle, by the silver windings of the river, traceable for miles, and reflecting the glowing hues of the sky by the venerable College of Eton, embowered in a grove of trees, and by a vast tract of well-wooded and well-cultivated country beyond it, interspersed with villages, churches, old halls, monasteries, and abbeys.

HARRISON AINSWORTH (1805–1882)

WINDSOR, with the winding River Thames, and the majestic castle in the distance, casts a powerful spell over the imagination. It is the principal residence of the sovereigns of Great Britain, and the photograph opposite (25607) shows the town and the magnificent castle from Clewer Path, where a young boy sits on the gate talking to two of his friends. Clearly visible are the Round Tower, St George's Chapel and the Curfew Tower. The flag flying over the castle could be the Royal Standard, indicating that members of the royal family are present.

William the Conqueror raised his keep on the castle hill in the 11th century. However, it was Edward III who brought romance to Windsor: his knights jousted in the upper ward and feasted in the Norman keep, and he revived Arthur's Round Table.

In photograph 53719 (below) a royal coach, followed by a contingent of Lifeguards, is seen coming down Castle Hill in 1906. A large crowd has gathered. The coach is possibly heading for St George's Chapel via the Henry VIII Gate. An inn on the right, now the Horse and Groom, has a board advertising 'Neville Reid and Co – Brewers to the King'.

A large contingent of Lifeguards is parading down Castle Hill (right, 66977). Queen Victoria gazes down regally from above, watching the proceedings.

Opposite:
WINDSOR, THE CASTLE FROM CLEWER PATH
1890 *25607p*

Above:
WINDSOR, CASTLE HILL
1914 *66977*

Left:
WINDSOR, CASTLE HILL
1906 *53719t*

THE predominant colour of the [throne] room is a rich blue. Everywhere we see the star of eight points silver and the cross of St George gules encircled with the garter and motto. The throne itself is of Indian workmanship with ivory carvings. The noble Order of the Garter was organised in this way: Edward III wanted a patron saint for England – for St Edward had never been popular with the Norman nobles. Such a saint had been discovered by Richard in the Crusades – St George, a victorious figure. Then Edward determined to found an order of St George, an entirely secular order, for the maintenance of chivalry.

VICTORIAN GUIDEBOOK

Windsor is majestic at all times, and will always look down with a lordly air on the surrounding country. VICTORIAN GUIDEBOOK

THE Van Dyck Room (bottom right, 36041) is so named because all the pictures to be seen on display have been painted by the artist Van Dyck. It is also known as the Queen's Ballroom. Here we see the room as it looked in 1895. Note the beautiful chandeliers and the two busts at the far end of the room.

New Knights and Ladies are invested with the insignia of the Order of the Garter in the Throne Room (opposite, 36037). The Garter Star can be seen in the ornate panels just above the doors.

The magnificent architecture of St George's Chapel (right, 35393) makes it one of the country's most impressive ecclesiastical buildings. It is the resting place of ten sovereigns, including Charles I. Henry VIII is buried next to Jane Seymour. This photograph brings to life the intricate designs and features that are to be seen in St George's Chapel. The choir sits in the lower tier of the choir stalls, military knights and lower clergy in the middle row, and the knights of the Garter and senior clergy in the upper tier. The banners of the knights remain in the chapel until death.

Opposite:
WINDSOR CASTLE,
THE THRONE ROOM
1895 *36037*

Left:
WINDSOR CASTLE,
ST GEORGE'S
CHAPEL 1895 *35393*

Below left:
WINDSOR CASTLE,
THE STATE
BEDROOM 1923
75190

Below right:
WINDSOR CASTLE,
THE VAN DYCK
ROOM 1895 *36041*

DOWN THE
RIVER THAMES

RIVER outings on the River Thames were so popular that in 1889 Jerome K Jerome embarked on one of the most famous boat trips in the history of English literature. His book 'Three Men in a Boat' recounts a quest for peace and quiet on the river. Jerome's narrator felt that he and his colleagues were 'overworked and in need of a rest'. Where better to go than the Thames, with its spacious reaches and tranquil backwaters?

The images on these pages convey the tranquillity Jerome was hoping to find. The photograph of Marlow (left, 47125) reveals the perfect haven for peaceful pottering. A rowing boat is approaching the lock, and the sun is shining beneficently down.

At Cookham (left, 77588), the Thames divides into three channels before turning south by chalk cliffs. This view is from Odney Common, an island along the north side of one of the channels, here named Lulle Brook. Families picnic on the banks of the river. A small child is feeding a swan.

Seen from the footbridge to the Oxfordshire bank (below, 52035), the eleven-arch bridge at Sonning is an 18th-century one that carries a vast amount of traffic. The Great House Hotel on the left is now much extended, and the church tower is largely concealed by more mature trees.

Opposite:
MARLOW, FROM THE
LOCK 1901 *47125t*

Above:
COOKHAM, ODNEY
COMMON 1925 *77588*

Left:
SONNING, THE BRIDGE
1904 *52035*

I HAVE stood and watched it, sometimes, when you could not see any water at all, but only a brilliant tangle of bright blazers, and gay caps, and saucy hats, and many-coloured parasols, and silken rugs, and cloaks, and streaming ribbons, and dainty whites; when looking down into the lock from the quay, you might fancy it was a huge box into which flowers of every hue and shade had been thrown pell-mell, and lay piled up in a rainbow heap, that covered every corner.

On a fine Sunday it presents this appearance nearly all day long, while, up the stream, and down the stream, lie, waiting their turn, outside the gates, long lines of still more boats; and boats are drawing near and passing away, so that the sunny river, from the Palace up to Hampton Church, is dotted and decked with yellow, and blue, and orange, and white, and red, and pink. All the inhabitants of Hampton and Moulsey dress themselves up in boating costume, and come and mouch round the lock with their dogs, and flirt, and smoke, and watch the boats.

JEROME K JEROME, 'THREE MEN IN A BOAT' 1889

Opposite far left:
MAIDENHEAD, BOULTERS LOCK
BRIDGE 1906 54082

Opposite near left:
MAIDENHEAD, BOULTERS LOCK
1906 54083

Above:
HENLEY, THE REGATTA 1890
27200

THE attendance of company on foot and afloat has never been exceeded – the mid-summer weather, no doubt, helping to swell the crowd. The number of pretty dresses might vie with those in the Royal Enclosure at Ascot, except perhaps for costliness, and the 'tout ensemble' as a spectacle has never been equalled. At the same time competitors seemed to play a secondary part in the days' proceedings, even if they were not voted a nuisance; picnics, luncheons, paddling about the course in row boats, and promenading up and down the meadows being apparently the great attraction. THE TIMES 1880

STOKE POGES

Buckinghamshire

Far from the madding crowd's ignoble strife …

SITUATED east of Stoke Park, the medieval church of Stoke Poges is famous beyond its architecture: this is reputedly the churchyard of Thomas Gray's 'Elegy Written in a Country Churchyard', one of the most well-known and well-loved of all English poems.

Gray was buried here in 1777 with his parents, near the brick Hastings Chapel of 1558, the left-hand gable in this view. The church underwent considerable change after this photograph was taken, and extensions to the north for a vestry and passageway were added in 1907. The spire, a timber replica built in 1831, was removed in 1924, and there is now a low pyramidal tiled roof in its stead. The creeper has now gone, exposing the Tudor brick of the Hastings Chapel on the left.

South-east of the churchyard, a path through a National Trust-owned copse winds to the fine memorial to Thomas Gray erected by his friend John Penn of Stoke Park in 1799. Designed by James Wyatt, it is a classical sarcophagus on a 20ft-high pedestal. The monument was deliberately designed this high so that it could be clearly seen from Penn's house. Indeed, Penn had the old vicarage demolished and relocated to provide an uninterrupted view. The pedestal panels are, not surprisingly, inscribed with lines from Gray's 'Ode on a Distant Prospect of Eton College' and his 'Elegy' – 'The paths of glory lead but to the grave'.

Opposite:
STOKE POGES, ST GILES'S CHURCH 1895 *35457*

THE CURFEW tolls the knell of parting day,
 The lowing herd winds slowly o'er the lea,
The ploughman homeward plods his weary way,
 And leaves the world to darkness and to me.

Now fades the glimmering landscape on the sight,
 And all the air a solemn stillness holds,
Save where the beetle wheels his droning flight,
 And drowsy tinklings lull the distant folds.

Save that from yonder ivy-mantled tower,
 The moping owl does to the moon complain,
Of such as wand'ring near her secret bower,
 Molest her ancient solitary reign.

Beneath those rugged elms, that yew-tree's shade,
 Where heaves the turf in many a mould'ring heap,
Each in his narrow cell for ever laid,
 The rude forefathers of the hamlet sleep.

The breezy call of incense-breathing morn,
 The swallow twittering from the straw-built shed,
The cock's shrill clarion, and the echoing horn,
 No more shall rouse them from their lowly bed.

For them no more the blazing hearth shall burn,
 Or busy housewife ply her evening care,
No children run to lisp their Sire's return,
 Nor climb his knees the envied kiss to share.

Oft did the harvest to their sickle yield,
 Their furrow oft the stubborn glebe has broke,
How jocund did they drive their team afield,
 How bowed the woods beneath their sturdy stoke!

Let not ambition mock their useful toil,
 Their homely joys and destiny obscure,
Nor grandeur hear with a disdainful smile,
 The short and simple annals of the poor.

The boast of heraldry, the pomp of power,
 And all that beauty, all that wealth e'er gave,
Awaits alike th'inevitable hour,
 The paths of glory lead but to the grave.

Nor you, ye proud, impute to these the fault,
 If mem'ry o'er their tomb no trophies raise,
Where, through the long-drawn aisle and fretted vault,
 The pealing anthem swells the note of praise.

Can storied urn, or animated bust,
 Back to its mansion call the fleeting breath?
Can honour's voice provoke the silent dust,
 Or flattery soothe the dull cold ear of death?

Perhaps in this neglected spot is laid,
 Some heart once pregnant with celestial fire,
Hands, that the rod of empire might have sway'd,
 Or waked to ecstasy the living lyre.

But knowledge to their eyes her ample page,
 Rich with the spoils of time did ne'er unroll,
Chill penury repress'd their noble rage,
 And froze the genial current of the soul.

Full many a gem of purest ray serene,
 The dark unfathom'd caves of ocean bear,
Full many a flower is born to blush unseen,
 And waste its sweetness on the desert air.

Some village Hampden, that with dauntless breast,
 The little tyrant of his fields withstood,
Some mute inglorious Milton here may rest,
 Some Cromwell, guiltless of his country's blood …

Far from the madding crowd's ignoble strife,
 Their sober wishes never learn'd to stray;
Along the cool sequester'd vale of life,
 They kept the noiseless tenour of their way …

BEAUTIFUL city! so venerable, so lovely, so unravaged by the fierce intellectual life of our century, so serene! … There are our young barbarians, all at play! And yet, steeped in sentiment as she lies, spreading her gardens to the moonlight, and whispering from her towers the last enchantments of the Middle Age, who will deny that Oxford, by her ineffable charm, keeps ever calling us nearer to the true goal of all of us, to the ideal, to perfection – to beauty, in a word, which is only truth seen from another side?

MATTHEW ARNOLD (1822–1888)

OXFORD
Oxfordshire

AT THE very heart of the county of Oxfordshire lies one of Britain's most beautiful cities. Likened by Thomas Hardy's Jude to 'the heavenly Jerusalem', Oxford's history, beauty and tradition are admired in every corner of the land. As a city it ranks in importance alongside Rome, Athens and Paris, and even when its scholars have left to make their mark in their world, they return again and again to embrace that curiously indefinable spirit of Oxford.

The city has a golden heart - a compact area of less than half a square mile in which the visitor will find a hugely varied assortment of ancient buildings, monuments and treasured landmarks which sit cheek by jowl with houses, shops and offices. In recent years millions of pounds have been spent on the city in restoring and cleaning the stonework of the colleges and university buildings, which had become grimy and black with the inevitable passage of time. Some were even in danger of disintegrating. The utmost care was taken in preserving them; today this great seat of learning, designed by distinguished architects such as Christopher Wren and Nicholas Hawksmoor, looks as good as it did when they helped to create it.

In view 45182 (left), St Mary the Virgin Church stands on the site of an 11th-century church which was once Oxford's most famous building. The present church includes a memorial to Dr John Radcliffe, one of the city's distinguished sons. Note how quiet the street is compared with today's modern traffic.

Opposite:
OXFORD, FROM MAGDALEN TOWER 1890 *26802*

Above:
OXFORD, HIGH STREET 1900 *45182p*

Left:
OXFORD, BALLIOL COLLEGE 1922 *72017*

Right:
OXFORD, MAGDALEN COLLEGE FROM THE RIVER 1922 *72005*

BLENHEIM PALACE
Oxfordshire

THE 'English Versailles' was built as a gift to the Duke of Marlborough after his victory over the French at Blenheim in 1704. Designed by Sir John Vanbrugh, its building was bedevilled with problems, including the Duke's fall from grace and a series of disputes between Vanbrugh and the Duchess which eventually caused Vanbrugh to resign.

On Vanbrugh's resignation, Nicholas Hawksmoor took over the building: among other features, he designed the doorways of the saloon (below, W250833) in white marble. The walls were painted by Louis Laguerre after it was decided that Sir James Thornhill's price of 25s per yard was too expensive.

The Long Library (opposite, W258041), which runs the entire length of the West Front, was still undecorated at the time of the Duke of Marlborough's death in 1722. Hawksmoor hired Isaac Mansfield to do the plasterwork.

Winston Churchill was born at Blenheim in 1874, but it was never his home, for the estate and title passed to his cousin, the ninth Duke.

AT Blenheim I took two very important decisions: to be born and to marry. I am happily content with the decisions I took on both those occasions.

WINSTON CHURCHILL (1874–1965)

Above:
BLENHEIM PALACE C1960 W258044

Left:
BLENHEIM PALACE, THE SALOON
C1960 W258033

Right:
BLENHEIM PALACE, SIR WINSTON
CHURCHILL'S BEDROOM C1960
W258029

Opposite:
BLENHEIM PALACE, THE LONG
LIBRARY C1960 W258041

THE library is a magnificent apartment occupying the western end of the house. The length of the room is 183 feet, and the fittings are of a sumptuous character.
It was originally designed as a picture gallery, but was afterwards filled with books in latticed cases, above which are suspended some family portraits. At the
upper end – to describe the library as it was before the late duke surrendered it to the auctioneer's hammer – is a marble statue of Queen Anne, 'under whose
auspices', as the inscription records, 'John, Duke of Marlborough, conquered, and to whose munificence he and his posterity with gratitude owe the possession
of Blenheim'. At the lower end is a bust of the general himself. The books, about 17,000 in number, were collected by Charles, third Earl of Sunderland.

VICTORIAN GUIDEBOOK

A 'nasty ill-looking place', full of 'East India plunderers, West Indian floggers, English tax-gorgers ... gluttons, drunkards and debauchers of all descriptions, female as well as male'.

WILLIAM COBBETT (1763–1835) ON CHELTENHAM

CHELTENHAM
Gloucestershire

CHELTENHAM adorns the borderland between the western escarpment of the Cotswolds and the broad plain of the Vale of Gloucester like some architectural jewel; it is a perfect Regency health spa, almost untouched at its heart by the unkind developments that ruined so many British towns during the 20th century. However, not everyone like it – read William Cobbett's impressions opposite.

The future spa town's first mineral spring was discovered in 1715 by a careful observer who had spent some time watching the watering habits of the local pigeons, who always seemed so fat and full of life. A pump room was constructed in 1738, and towards the end of the 18th century King George III gave the growing town the royal seal of approval by bringing his family to take the waters. Business boomed; and when the town of Cheltenham Spa became a city, its grateful citizens incorporated a pigeon into its crest.

Cheltenham's long Promenade (59033 and 73481), with its stylish buildings, became one of the town's most fashionable residential areas when the spa town began to spread away from the vicinity of the High Street and the old town. The Neptune Fountain (73485) has adorned the top end of the Promenade since 1893, when it was built as part of a project to improve the ambience of this long avenue. Cheltenham's Borough Surveyor, Mr Hall, undertook the design of the fountain, and had the new fountain made from Portland stone; he was supposedly inspired by Rome's Trevi Fountain.

Opposite:
CHELTENHAM,
THE PROMENADE 1923   *73481t*

Left:
CHELTENHAM,
THE PROMENADE 1907   *59033*

Above:
CHELTENHAM, THE
PROMENADE FOUNTAINS 1923
73485

Right:
CHELTENHAM, THE UPPER
PROMENADE 1901   *47264*

CHELTENHAM College was originally a private concern, with shareholders who were able to nominate potential pupils. Many of the early pupils were the sons of army officers, who intended to graduate into a military career. Cheltenham's reputation as an educational centre really started in 1841 with the establishment of the Boys' College. By this period, Cheltenham had already become a much-frequented spa town in which many Victorians had taken up permanent residence.

Even today, the college boasts an annual summer cricket festival in the best public school tradition. Apart from the clothes worn by the spectators, the scenes in the photograph (59038) could have been taken at any time during the last century. In the background is the college chapel, designed and built by H A Prothero to great critical acclaim. Earlier college students had worshipped at Christ Church in the town.

Above left: CHELTENHAM, HIGH STREET 1901 *47265p*

Below left: CHELTENHAM, HIGH STREET 1906 *54320*

Right: CHELTENHAM, THE BOYS' COLLEGE PLAYING FIELDS 1907 *59038p*

THE COTSWOLDS

Gloucestershire, Oxfordshire

At weekends in summer and on Bank Holidays, Bourton on the Water has to suffer the invasions which have resulted from the discovery of its beauty. GUIDEBOOK 1924

THIS is country at its most pastoral: a landscape of rolling hills and meadows, quiet river banks, honey-coloured stone villages and bustling market towns. So attractive are they that many of towns and villages were overrun during summer weekends even as far back as the 1920s. Bourton-on-the-Water's accessibility from the towns and cities of the Midlands has made it a favourite day out. Yet it is still possible to find a quiet corner to feed the ducks (above right, B392047). Bourton Bridge, which carries the busy main road past the village, was the first of the many bridges here; the original structure dated back to Roman times, and was designed to aid the legions as they marched down the Fosse Way.

Burford (left, B369011) is a picturesque Cotswold town in Oxfordshire lying on the slope of a steep hill above the Windrush valley about 20 miles east of Cheltenham. In the broad High Street old inns, houses, small shops and buildings jostle in a medley of complementary styles. Beyond the war memorial in this view we glimpse the spire of St John the Baptist's Church, where during the Civil War some 340 troops from the Parliamentarian army were held prisoner.

Broadway (below right, 44113) is a tempting village for tourists. From about 1600 it was a thriving staging post, and horse-drawn carriages by the dozen stopped here to feed and water en route from London to Worcester – a journey of more than 17 hours. Over 30 inns offered passengers refreshment and accommodation. The long, very beautiful street is lined with historic buildings, from humble cottages to fine houses, all in harmonious vernacular styles.

Opposite:
BURFORD, HIGH STREET C1955 *B369011*

Above right:
BOURTON-ON-THE-WATER, FEEDING THE DUCKS C1955 *B392047*

Below right:
BROADWAY, THE VILLAGE 1899 *44113*

THE village of Slad (left, 62708) sits in one of the loveliest valleys in Gloucestershire. Its most famous son was the author and poet Laurie Lee, who was born in Stroud in 1914 and moved to Slad when he was three. He recalled his childhood in his celebrated book 'Cider With Rosie'. At the age of 19, Lee walked to London, then on to civil war-stricken Spain. His memories are captured in 'As I Walked Out One Midsummer Morning'.

'Chipping' means 'market' in Old English, and Chipping Campden (below left, C335034) gained its affluence as a market centre for the local woollen industry. The town boasts many fine stone buildings, including some 17th-century almshouses, a colonnaded Market Hall, and St James's Church, one of the most magnificent ecclesiastical buildings in the region.

In Bibury (below, B530002) is one of the most picturesque – and most photographed – groups of cottages in the Cotswolds. Arlington Row's first function was as a barn. Then in the 17th century the building was converted into home-workers' cottages for weavers in the wool trade. Arlington Row is now owned by the National Trust. The River Coln played an essential role in Bibury's development. From Saxon times it provided the motive power for local corn and cloth mills, in addition to feeding the local system of water meadows, which were made fertile by regular flooding. Bibury is a well-spread-out settlement. This is because it was formed from a number of tiny hamlets and individual properties that gradually grew together over the centuries.

A Summer Evening Churchyard
Lechlade, Gloucestershire

THE wind has swept from the wide atmosphere
    Each vapour that obscured the sunset's ray,
And pallid Evening twines its beaming hair
    In duskier braids around the languid eyes of Day:
Silence and Twilight, unbeloved of men,
Creep hand in hand from yon obscurest glen.

They breathe their spells towards the departing day,
    Encompassing the earth, air, stars, and sea;
Light, sound, and motion, own the potent sway,
    Responding to the charm with its own mystery.
The winds are still, or the dry church-tower grass
Knows not their gentle motions as they pass.

Thou too, aerial pile, whose pinnacles
    Point from one shrine like pyramids of fire,
Obey'st I in silence their sweet solemn spells,
    Clothing in hues of heaven thy dim and distant spire,
Around whose lessening and invisible height
Gather among the stars the clouds of night.

The dead are sleeping in their sepulchres:
    And, mouldering as they sleep, a thrilling sound,
Half sense half thought, among the darkness stirs,
    Breathed from their wormy beds all living things around,
And, mingling with the still night and mute sky,
Its awful hush is felt inaudibly.

Thus solemnized and softened, death is mild
    And terrorless as this serenest night.
Here could I hope, like some enquiring child
    Sporting on graves, that death did hide from human sight
Sweet secrets, or beside its breathless sleep
That loveliest dreams perpetual watch did keep.

    PERCY BYSSHE SHELLEY (1792–1822)

THE MALVERNS
Worcestershire

'THE Vision Concerning Piers the Plowman' by William Langland was inspired by the Malvern Hills, and remains one of the most important early works of English literature, with its vivid portrayal of 14th-century life. On a fine and clear day it is not hard to recapture the 'Vision' from the summit of the hills. Wyndspoint (left, 7071b) was once the home of the singer and musical patron Jenny Lind, the 'Swedish Nightingale'.

Great Malvern town is set against the stunning backdrop of the Malvern Hills, that great range of summits that rises above the surrounding plains of Worcestershire; they form one of the finest ridge walks in England, with extensive views all the way across the Midlands, the Border Marches and Wales.

In 1899, Edward Elgar rented Craeg Lea (below, 51150), which commanded wonderful views of the Malvern range. Here he composed some of his most popular works, including 'The Dream of Gerontius' and 'Pomp and Circumstance'. The Elgars used to raise a Union Jack if they required the services of a local taxi, a horse-drawn brake, which did the round trip across the hills each day.

Opposite:
THE MALVERN RANGE AND WYNDSPOINT FROM THE CAMP HILL C1900 *7071b*

Above left:
GREAT MALVERN, THE VIEW NEAR IVY SCAR 1923 *73734p*

Below left:
GREAT MALVERN, FROM THE CHURCH TOWER 1899 *43987*

Below right:
CRAEG LEA, WELLS ROAD 1904 *51150*

WILLIAM Shakespeare was born in a house in Henley Street, Stratford-upon-Avon, on 23 April 1564. In his day the building was really two houses: one where the family lived, the other where John Shakespeare worked as a glover and wool merchant. The walls were, and to some extent still are, covered with the signatures of visitors, though a great many have been whitewashed over. Some visitors even scratched their names on the window panes. Among the signatures are those of Sir Walter Scott, Thomas Carlyle, Robert Browning and William Makepeace Thackeray.

AFTER *wandering through two or three streets, I found my way to Shakespeare's birthplace, which is almost a smaller and humbler house than any description can prepare the visitor to expect ... The portion of the edifice with which Shakespeare had anything to do is hardly large enough, in the basement, to contain the butcher's stall that one of his descendants kept, and that still remains there, windowless, with the cleaver-cuts in its hacked counter, which projects into the street under a little penthouse roof, as if waiting for a new occupant ... Thence I was ushered upstairs to the room in which Shakespeare is supposed to have been born; though, if you peep too curiously into the matter, you may find the shadow of an ugly doubt on this, as well as most other points of his mysterious life. It is the chamber over the butcher's shop, and is lighted by one broad window containing a great many small, irregular panes of glass ... So low it is, that I could easily touch the ceiling, and might have done so without a tiptoe stretch, had it been a good deal higher.*

NATHANIEL HAWTHORNE (1804–864)

SHAKESPEARE'S STRATFORD

Warwickshire

STRATFORD-UPON-AVON is where William Shakespeare was born, and is the most visited place in England apart from London.

It was in the room shown below right (31061), noted for its low ceiling, that William Shakespeare is said to have been born. In 1892 the room was almost bare, with dirty and discoloured plaster.

The village of Shottery, just one mile from Stratford, is where Shakespeare chose to do his courting. Anne Hathaway was the eldest of the three daughters of John Hathaway, a farmer. She was eight years older than William; he was only 18 when they married. Her cottage is shown below left (31084).

WILLIAM SHAKESPEARE
(1564–1616)

Opposite:
STRATFORD-UPON-AVON, SHAKESPEARE'S BIRTHPLACE c1850
S21601

Left:
SHOTTERY, ANNE HATHAWAY'S COTTAGE 1892 31084

Right:
STRATFORD-UPON-AVON, SHAKESPEARE'S BIRTHROOM 1892
31061

WARWICK
Warwickshire

WARWICK is situated in the heart of England. Though probably the least spoilt of all the English county towns, little survives of pre-1694 Warwick. In that year much of the town centre was destroyed by fire.

Lord Leycester's Hospital (right, 31022), was built in 1571, and provided accommodation for 12 poor brothers, former soldiers who had seen service with the Leycester family. They were required to wear a blue gown and the silver badge of the Bear and Ragged Staff of the Warwick earldom.

The Warwick Arms area (opposite, 72343) is always a busy part of the town. In the hotel's heyday, there was stabling for 70 horses at the rear. The glass canopy has now gone, but the bunch of grapes above remains.

A quiet, old-fashioned, fairly prosperous town, with a sufficient, but not excessive, amount of trade – in short, a typical country town. VICTORIAN GUIDEBOOK

Above:
WARWICK,
THE LORD
LEYCESTER HOSPITAL
1892 *31022*

Right:
WARWICK,
ST JOHN'S 1892
31031

Opposite:
WARWICK,
HIGH STREET 1922
72343t

WARWICK Castle is so frequently visited that it needs little description. The winding road, cut out of the solid rock from the lodge to the castle gate, is a fitting approach to the stately fortress-palace, and well prepares the visitor for what is to follow. Some will prefer to traverse the gardens, so far as watchful custodians permit, turning aside to the solid-looking Gothic conservatory to see the great Warwick vase, brought from fair Tivoli; others will follow the courteous housekeeper down the long suite of castle halls, noting the glorious views from the deep embayed windows, duly admiring the bed in which Queen Anne once slept, with the portrait of her majesty, plump and rubicund, on the opposite wall. The logs heaped up, as logs have been for centuries, in readiness for the great hall fire, carry the mind back to olden fashions; the inlaid table of precious stones, said to have been worth ten thousand pounds, but recently injured by some silly tourist, excites a languid curiosity.

THE REVEREND SAMUEL MANNING C1885

Left:
WARWICK, THE CASTLE ENTRANCE 1892 *31007*

Opposite top:
WARWICK, CAESAR'S TOWER AND GUY'S TOWER 1922 *72366*

Opposite left:
WARWICK, THE CASTLE 1892 *31001*

Opposite right:
WARWICK, GUY'S CLIFFE, THE HOUSE FROM THE RIVER 1892 *31037*

THE earliest fortifications at Warwick were thrown up in AD 915 by Ethelfleda of Mercia, the daughter of Alfred the Great. The ditch and palisade defences were placed round the town itself, Warwick at this time being little more than a frontier town next to the Danelaw. Ethelfleda joined with her brother Edward the Elder to reconquer English territory held by the Danes. In 917 she took Derby, and the following year captured Leicester.

Henry de Newburgh built a large wooden motte and bailey on the site of the present castle, and before his death in 1123 he might well have begun to replace the wood with stone. During the Barons' War, Warwick Castle was sacked and all but destroyed by forces loyal to Simon de Montfort.

Begun in 1751, Guy's Cliffe House (below right, 31037) was added to later, before becoming a ruin in the mid 20th century. Considerable fire damage was caused whilst a Sherlock Holmes film was being shot here some years ago - the building had to be restored to the ruined state it was in before the fire! A former housemaid, Sarah Kemble, eloped from here one morning and married her sweetheart William. She took to the stage and became the famous actress Sarah Siddons. In later years she became a welcome guest in the house where she had once been a maid.

And he began already to be proud of being a Rugby boy, as he passed the schoolgates, with the oriel window above.

'TOM BROWN'S SCHOOLDAYS'

Right:
RUGBY, THE CLOCK
TOWER AND
ST ANDREW'S
CHURCH 1922
72125t

Opposite above:
RUGBY, SCHOOL
HOUSE C1955
R69026

Opposite below:
RUGBY, RUGBY
SCHOOL 1922 *72123*

90

'AND so here's Rugby, sir, at last, and you'll be in plenty of time for dinner at the School-house, as I told you,' said the old guard, pulling his horn out of its case and tootle-tooting away, while the coachman shook up his horses, and carried them along the side of the school close, round Dead-man's corner, past the school-gates, and down the High Street to the Spread Eagle, the wheelers in a spanking trot, and leaders cantering, in a style which would not have disgraced "Cherry Bob", 'ramping, stamping, tearing, swearing Billy Harwood', or any other of the old coaching heroes.

Tom's heart beat quick as he passed the great schoolfield or close, with its noble elms, in which several games at football were going on, and tried to take in at once the long line of gray buildings, beginning with the chapel, and ending with the School-house, the residence of the head-master, where the great flag was lazily waving from the highest round tower. And he began already to be proud of being a Rugby boy, as he passed the schoolgates, with the oriel window above, and saw the boys standing there, looking as if the town belonged to them, and nodding in a familiar manner to the coachman, as if any one of them would be quite equal to getting on the box, and working the team down street as well as he.

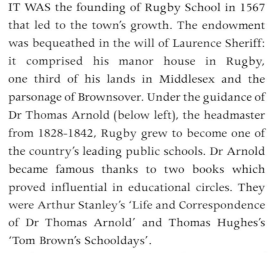

THOMAS HUGHES (1822–1896), 'TOM BROWN'S SCHOOLDAYS'

IT WAS the founding of Rugby School in 1567 that led to the town's growth. The endowment was bequeathed in the will of Laurence Sheriff: it comprised his manor house in Rugby, one third of his lands in Middlesex and the parsonage of Brownsover. Under the guidance of Dr Thomas Arnold (below left), the headmaster from 1828-1842, Rugby grew to become one of the country's leading public schools. Dr Arnold became famous thanks to two books which proved influential in educational circles. They were Arthur Stanley's 'Life and Correspondence of Dr Thomas Arnold' and Thomas Hughes's 'Tom Brown's Schooldays'.

The town is famous for the 'exploit of William Webb Ellis', a pupil of Rugby School, who in 1823 carried the ball and ran with it during a soccer match. And so the game of rugby was born.

SHREWSBURY
Shropshire

THE timber houses here were built by wealthy merchants in the late 1500s. They were wool merchants, and it was their trade that made medieval Shrewsbury one of the richest towns in England. As time went by the wool trade was replaced by the cloth trade, and to this day evidence of the wealth of these merchants can be seen in the many glorious timber buildings throughout the region. Therefore, R Maddox & Co (opposite, 73810) is continuing a tradition by selling cloth and clothing.

Frankwell (below right, 63256) was one of the town's earliest suburbs, dating from straight after the Norman conquest. This building still exists, but not in Shropshire. It was an inn known as the String of Horses and was taken to the Avoncroft Museum in Bromsgrove and re-erected to make way for a roundabout.

Once named Candle Lane because candles were sold there (above right, 63226), this street was renamed to commemorate the visit of Princess Victoria in the 1800s. The market hall dates from the reign of Queen Elizabeth I, and was used as a corn and produce market on the ground floor and a cloth market upstairs.

Today there is a footbridge crossing the Severn at this point (below, 63218). Notice how the ferryman is hauling on the rope to carry his passengers across the river. The fare was 1s 2d.

Below left:
SHREWSBURY, THE BOAT HOUSE INN AND THE FERRY 1911 *63218t*

Left:
SHREWSBURY, OLD MARKET HALL AND PRINCESS STREET 1911 *63226*

Below:
SHREWSBURY, FRANKWELL 1911 *63256*

Opposite:
SHREWSBURY, HIGH STREET 1923 *73810*

[SHREWSBURY'S] old buildings have a skeleton of oak, filled up with brick, plaster, or other material, and with the beams of the timber marked out in black paint; besides which, in houses of any pretension, there are generally trefoils, and other Gothic-looking ornaments, likewise painted black. They have an indescribable charm for me – the more, I think, because they are wooden – but, indeed, I cannot tell why it is that I like them so well, and am never tired of looking at them. A street was a development of human life, in the days when these houses were built; whereas a modern street is but the cold plan of an architect, without individuality or character, and without the human emotion which a man kneads into the walls which he builds on a scheme of his own ...

NATHANIEL HAWTHORNE (1804–1864)

93

I CAME upon the hill above the Severn; and descended, upon crack'd pitchers, amidst iron forges to the iron bridge … I breakfasted upon a nice hot roll … and then seated myself upon the river's bank, whose water is very low. It is now nine years since I rode this way … any tourist may observe the diminution of the woods and timber and how, yearly, the country becomes bare and woodless.

JOHN BYNG JULY 1793

THE boat in this picture, probably a shallow draft Severn trow, would have attracted little or no attention from the locals. Not so in 1787. The village was buzzing with excitement as crowds gathered to watch ironmaster John Wilkinson make a fool of himself. He had announced his intention to launch an iron boat onto the Severn near the bridge. Everyone knew iron was heavier than water, so the boat must sink. However, it didn't!

Many people avoided paying the tolls on the bridge by rowing coracles across the river. It was here, too, that a boy named Matthew Webb learnt to swim. He was later to become the first man to swim the English Channel in 1875. He later tried to swim across the Niagara Falls, but was caught in a current and dragged under. His body was found four days later.

Today, the area around Ironbridge is a World Heritage site. Many of the old workshops and factories are being restored or converted into museums. These include the Blist's Hill Museum, (with many restored buildings), a museum of iron, a china museum, a tile-making museum, and even a restored police station.

IRONBRIDGE
Shropshire

ABRAHAM DARBY probably chose Coalbrookdale for the location of his ironworks because there were local sources of coal and iron ore, and sufficient water power to work the bellows of his blast furnace. Darby was also able to export his products by way of the Severn. He was smelting with coke as early as 1709, yet it would be over fifty years before other ironmasters followed suit. Largely financed by Quaker merchants from Bristol, the Coalbrookdale works became famous in 1779 when Abraham Darby II manufactured the castings for this, the first bridge in the world to be made of iron. Weighing 380 tons, the single-arched structure, with a span of 100 feet and overall length of 196 feet, was floated down the River Severn in sections and assembled in situ without obstructing other river traffic. The place where the bridge was erected was named after it: Ironbridge.

The photograph below left (30892) affords us a view across Ironbridge. Here we get an idea of just how steep the limestone slopes are upon which the town is built, and how narrow the gorge is through which the river flows.

Water power played an important role in the development of the factory system (below right, 30898), for it was harnessed to drive machinery in cotton and woollen mills alike. Water was also used for pumping and lifting in mines and for crushing ore, and Abraham Darby used vast amounts of water to work the bellows of his blast furnace at Coalbrookdale.

Opposite:
IRONBRIDGE 1892 *30891*

Left:
IRONBRIDGE, FROM THE ROTUNDA 1892 *30892*

Above:
IRONBRIDGE, THE BRIDGE 1904 *51376*

Right:
IRONBRIDGE, THE WATERWHEEL 1892 *30898*

STAFFORDSHIRE

STAFFORDSHIRE has a rich heritage of old-established industries. It is most celebrated for its Wedgwood pottery. How long pottery has been manufactured in the county is open to debate, but by the 10th century it was already being made in and around Stafford.

In the 14th century forges were established at Cannock, Rugeley and Sedgley to smelt iron ore. Water wheels provided the motive power, but it was in the 18th century that the industry made great advances when John Wilkinson established the first coke-fired smelter at Bradley.

Mining, too, was a significant industry, and by the 17th century 50,000 tonnes of coal were being produced annually. Brewing has always been vital to Staffordshire's economy, centred on Burton upon Trent. Industry would not have prospered without good communications, and early on Josiah Wedgwood had the foresight to encourage the building of the Trent & Mersey Canal, which allowed flint and china clay to be easily carried to the potteries at Burslem and finished goods to be transported in bulk to the port of Liverpool.

Left:
LEEK, MARKET PLACE C1955 *L379007t*

Below left:
BURSLEM, GENERAL VIEW 1956 *B303002*

Opposite:
ABBOTS BROMLEY, THE HORN DANCE C1955 *A165385*

IT has everything that England has, including thirty miles of Watling Street; and England can show nothing more beautiful and nothing uglier than the works of nature and the works of man to be seen within the limits of the county. It is England in little, lost in the midst of England, unsung by searchers after the extreme; perhaps occasionally somewhat sore at this neglect, but how proud in the instinctive cognizance of its representative features and traits!

ARNOLD BENNETT (1867–1931)

A STAFFORDSHIRE FLAT BACK SCOTTISH BOWER GROUP *ZZZ04626*

A PAIR OF VICTORIAN STAFFORDSHIRE SPANIELS *ZZZ04625*

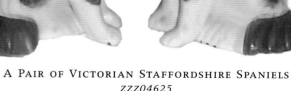

Photographs courtesy of Torridge Auctions, Bideford, Devon

THE Abbots Bromley Horn Dance ritual dates back as far as 1226 - it was performed at the three-day Barthelmy Fair in that year. However, it is believed to be much older than that, and has survived down the centuries, continuing to flourish today in this Staffordshire village.

The great horns themselves are 1,000 years old - they have been carbon dated. The dance is performed on Wakes Monday. The horns are collected from the church in the morning, and carried aloft, the dancers performing their ritual to music played on a melodeon. The dancers – six Deer-men, a Fool, Hobby Horse, Bowman and Maid Marian – carry the horns around the village, stopping traffic and performing the dance many times. They trek up to ten miles, threading a path between the outlying farms and houses. Meanwhile, a jester strikes people in the crowd with a pig's bladder, which is said to encourage fertility.

THE canals of England are a well-kept secret. We drive over a hump-backed bridge and sometimes catch a fleeting glimpse of a smooth filament of water and possibly the heavy balance beam of a lock. We may spot a brightly painted narrow boat chugging gently onwards, yet canals do not impinge much on our daily lives. They run more often than not through the back yards of our towns and cities. However, for a period of our history they were vital arteries connecting major industrial centres. There was once a huge network of them covering the country, joining north to south and east to west. Pioneering giants like Telford and Brindley forged level waterways through seemingly impossible terrain. Without them the Industrial Revolution would never have got off the ground. Yet by the early years of the 20th century they had declined in importance, and many had fallen into dereliction.

In the photograph opposite (70492) we see two horse-drawn narrowboats, 'Linnet' and 'Evelyn', at the attractively-sited lock in Cassiobury Park, Watford. This was just one lock in the long climb from the west edge of London up the Chilterns: 25 miles and 42 locks on the Grand Junction Canal (later to become part of the Grand Union), the original main transport artery between London and Birmingham.

Below the second Tyrley lock on the Shropshire Union Canal near Market Drayton, a loaded narrowboat poses for the camera. This boat is probably a 'number one', the owner having just a single horse and his own boat. The horse is deep in his nosebag, enjoying a feed after the long haul through the lock. The man would be working the locks, the little girl driving the horse and the mother steering: this was a family business. Bargemen worked 6- or 7-day weeks, received no sick pay, and no salary during freeze-ups.

Opposite:
WATFORD, CASSIOBURY PARK AND THE CANAL LOCK 1921 *70492t*

Left:
MARKET DRAYTON, TYRLEY LOCKS 1911 *63346*

TWO great canals forge a route into the heart of England from the south. The Grand Union is an amalgamation of several older waterways. From the Thames at Brentford it journeys north towards Birmingham, linking many important industrial and commercial centres. The Oxford Canal has always been a poor neighbour, yet it creates a vital long-distance link with the rest of the Midlands network, and with the Coventry Canal.

The Oxford Canal (left, C291006) was first opened in 1778. Passing through much remote and beautiful countryside, it is a classic example of contour cutting by the engineer Samuel Simcock. There are no locks because the canal hugs the contours of the land with much twisting and wriggling. Here at Cropredy we are witness to a waterside idyll. A houseboat created from a converted narrow boat serves as an inexpensive home. Ducks paddle alongside.

In the photograph left (H428501) is a breasted-up pair of narrow boats owned by Thomas Clayton of Oldbury. We are probably just below Copper Mill Lock at Harefield on the Grand Union Canal. The pair of horse boats, of which the 'Blyth' is the left-hand one, is heading towards the bank, where the man in the bow will heave his line to the shore for the horse to be re-attached. Clayton's boats specialised in carrying waste products of the gas industry. Note the bargewoman in traditional long dress, pinafore and white head shawl.

Above left:
CROPREDY, THE OXFORD CANAL
c1960 *C291006*

Below left:
HAREFIELD, CANAL BOATS c1930
H428501

Above:
BANBURY, THE OXFORD CANAL
1921 70593

HERE we see another peaceful scene. The 'Doris' is a disused butty, and makes a fine perch for the anglers. The silence they are obviously enjoying has gone now: it has been shattered by the construction of the M40 motorway close by. No photograph could better depict the incomparable power of the countryside canal to conjure up peace and contentment, with its tree-fringed towpath and surrounding meadows. Anglers sit gazing dreamily at their floats from the rotting hulk.

CONSTABLE COUNTRY
Suffolk

HOW much I wish I had been with you on your fishing excursion in the New Forest! What river can it be? But the sound of water escaping from mill-dams, etc., willows, old rotten planks, flimsy posts and brickwork, I love such things … As long as I do paint, I shall never cease to paint such places. They have always been my delight, and I should indeed have been delighted in seeing what you describe, and in your company, 'in the company of a man to whom nature does not spread her volume in vain'. Still I should paint my own places best; painting is with me but another word for feeling, and I associate my 'careless boyhood' with all that lies on the banks of the Stour; those scenes made me a painter, and I am grateful.

JOHN CONSTABLE (1776–1837)

I associate my 'careless boyhood' with all that lies on the banks of the Stour; those scenes made me a painter, and I am grateful. JOHN CONSTABLE

JOHN CONSTABLE is England's quintessential landscape painter. He has made the gentle rolling fields around Dedham Vale his own. His father, Golding, a miller, owned mills at Dedham and Flatford, and two windmills at East Bergholt.

Golding wanted him to follow in the family business, but with encouragement from his mother, John went to London to study art, eventually gaining a place at the Royal Academy. Although his early commissions were not to his own taste, he persevered with painting the countryside where he was brought up around Dedham Vale, in a style which at the time was not generally acceptable.

When 'The Hay Wain' was first shown in the Royal Academy in 1818, it received a response which was luke-warm, to say the least. In Paris, where impressionist painting had already taken off, he was feted as a celebrity, and was awarded a gold medal by the King of France. His work only received recognition at home later on.

Beside the quiet mill-pond at Flatford Mill stands Willy Lott's Cottage, instantly recognisable as the setting for Constable's famous painting 'The Hay Wain'. Willy Lott, the mill-hand, is reputed to have lived in this cottage for 88 years. Flatford Mill, built in 1733, featured in several of Constable's works.

Opposite:
FLATFORD, WILLY LOTT'S COTTAGE 1907 *57554*

Above:
FLATFORD, BRIDGE HOUSE AND THE STOUR C1960 *F31051*

Left:
FLATFORD, BRIDGE COTTAGE 1907 *57552*

Right:
FLATFORD, CONSTABLE'S LANE 1907 *57555*

Southwold remains a quiet, sleepy, picturesque, and wholly delightful retreat, innocent alike of piers and minstrels, of ugly terraces, and of those indications of 'life' which induce lovers of peace and the picturesque to fly in dismay from popular resorts by the sea. [It] charms the visitor whose soul does not pine for a brass band and a general uproar.

Victorian Guide

THE SUFFOLK COAST

Suffolk

CRUMBLING sandy cliffs and shingle beaches, ancient and now rare lowland heaths, creeks of glistening mud, and salt marshes that attract innumerable birds - clearly this is an area of outstanding natural beauty, and it was officially designated as such thirty years ago. Even the looming presence of the Sizewell nuclear power station cannot detract from the visual appeal of this area, and indeed one must admire the courage and confidence of those planners who placed it on Britain's most fragile and vulnerable coast.

Although it can mesmerise with its dramatic beauty, the sea is not always an object of affection here. It has been too fickle a neighbour, often tearing at the land in the most predatory manner. It swept away the great port and town of Dunwich in the Middle Ages.

At the exquisite seaside town of Southwold (left, 38620), the crowded beach reminds us of the importance of the sea in the economy and the lives of its inhabitants. The characteristic clinker-built, double-ended beach yawls, the speediest craft on the east coast, competed with each other to off-load cargoes from larger ships offshore. Here sails and also, it seems, fishing nets are drying.

There has been a ferry across the River Blyth at Walberswick for over 800 years, and between 1885 and 1942 it was the rather primitive chain ferry, which we see here (below left, 69126), carrying a horse and cart across to the Southwold side. This one is steam-operated. Today, as in the 13th century, a rowing boat provides the service for a modest fee. So, in this case, times do not change!

Opposite:
SOUTHWOLD,
THE BEACH 1919
69118t

Above:
SOUTHWOLD,
THE BEACH 1896
38620

Left:
WALBERSWICK,
THE FERRY 1919
69126

THE Regency fashion for sea bathing was the start of Aldeburgh's improved outlook (above, 56816). After the railway had reached the town, it helped to sustain the economy. There were still nearly 200 licensed fishing vessels in Aldeburgh at this time, catching herrings and sprats and sole. Between these working boats sprawled on the shingle, bathing huts were appearing, and the two trades, fishing and tourism, lived peacefully together. The town found still greater celebrity when Benjamin Britten, who lived here, set up the now internationally-known Aldeburgh Festival.

The story of the demise of Dunwich (opposite, 62044), in medieval times a prosperous port until the ravages of the North Sea gradually demolished its soft, sandy cliffs, is one of the most romantic of the Suffolk coast. There were still substantial remains of the parish church on the clifftop above the beach tents when this photograph was taken. A substantial shingle beach this may be, but it offers no protection to the soft substance of the cliffs. All Saints' Church now stands at the edge, soon to join the lost medieval town in a watery grave. In recent years, divers have probed the sea bed and located ruins in the murky deep.

Above: ALDEBURGH, THE PARADE 1906 *56816*

Opposite: DUNWICH, THE BEACH 1909 *62044*

I DEFY any one, at desolate, exquisite Dunwich, to be disappointed in anything ... Dunwich is not even the ghost of its dead self; almost all you can say of it is that it consists of the mere letters of its old name. The coast, up and down, for miles, has been, for more centuries than I presume to count, gnawed away by the sea. All the grossness of its positive life is now at the bottom of the German Ocean, which moves for ever, like a ruminating beast, an insatiable, indefatigable lip. Few things are so melancholy – and so redeemed from mere ugliness by sadness – as this long, artificial straightness that the monster has impartially maintained. If at low tide you walk on the shore, the cliffs, of little height, show you a defence picked as bare as a bone; and you can say nothing kinder of the general humility and general sweetness of the land than that this sawlike action gives it, for the fancy, an interest, a sort of mystery, that more than makes up for what it may have surrendered ...

The biggest items are of course the two ruins, the great church and its tall tower, now quite on the verge of the cliff, and the crumbled, ivied wall of the immense cincture of the Priory.

HENRY JAMES 1897

THE Norfolk Broads have been a watery playground for holidaymakers for decades. It is hard to believe that these wide expanses of smooth water are man-made. In medieval times peat was dug on a grand scale and the landscape would have appeared very different. The diggings were originally dry, resembling great open-cast mines, and were prone to flooding and inundation during periods of rising water levels.

In the view of Potter Heigham (left, P167052) the crew of the boat in the foreground have lowered the mast, ready to thread a course under the 14th-century bridge, which has a headroom of only seven feet. Another craft, a pleasure cruiser (bottom left, 86381), has lowered its mast to enable it to pass under the stone and brick bridge with its wide central arch and two pointed side arches. It was a matter of pride amongst traditional boatmen - and required immense skill – to approach the bridge at full speed, reef the sail, lower the mast and emerge the other side without losing way. Potter Heigham is an important village, as it bridges the river Thurne. It has become a major centre for boat building and hiring.

Ludham (below, L110082), sits on higher ground, which in Broadland can be just a few feet above sea level. The flat lands around are threaded by three great rivers, the Thurne, the Ant and the Bure. The old windpump at Turf Fen, its sails now still, offers testament to man's continual battle with the rising waters.

Above left: POTTER HEIGHAM, THE RIVER THURNE C1926 *P167052*

Below left: POTTER HEIGHAM, THE BRIDGE 1934 *86381*

Below: LUDHAM, AN OLD WINDPUMP C1955 *L110082*

Above:
HORNING, ON THE BROADS 1902
48108

WHEN sailing a wherry you had to be able to sail very close to the wind, for the narrow waterways allowed no extravagant tacking manoeuvres. It was unwise to touch bottom either, especially when the boat was low in the water and loaded with freight. Built of oak, the gaff-rigged wherry was precisely designed for Broadland conditions, and fleets of them once plied between Yarmouth and Norwich.

Norwich is (as you please) either a city in an orchard, or an orchard in a city, so equally are houses and trees blended into it, so that the pleasures of the country and the populousness of the city meet here together.

THOMAS FULLER, WORTHIES OF ENGLAND 1662

BY THE banks of the graceful River Wensum is the 15th-century gateway to the city's diminutive canal (above, 28157p), which penetrates a course through to the very margins of the cathedral. Along this waterway medieval bargemen hauled the Caen stone used in the construction of the lofty spire and walls. The watergate was restored in the late 1940s. Pull's Ferry was named after a 19th-century ferryman.

Elm Hill (opposite, 81806) was rescued from slum clearance by the Norwich Society in 1927 and beautifully restored. Seeing it now, the intended vandalism is difficult to comprehend. In the 16th and 17th centuries the street echoed to the hum of cloth looms. The buildings then became overcrowded housing for the woollen industry's factory workers and, after 1850, for shoe-factory workers. Now no longer a pub, the Britons Arms on the left of the photograph, built as a community of religious women in the 15th century, was the only house to survive a great fire in 1507.

NORWICH
Norfolk

THERE is a spacious air about Norwich, the capital of Norfolk and 'city of churches' (there were once 56). At its heart are a great cattle market and two magnificent buildings, the cathedral and the castle, both Norman in origin. Parts of Norwich's old medieval walls are still standing, and this deepens its atmosphere of history and tradition.

The cathedral (below, 28147) is essentially Norman, and only the great late 15th-century spire has materially changed distant views. It soars to 315 ft, the second highest spire in England after Salisbury. Its predecessor had been blown through the choir roof in a great gale in 1362, which also resulted in the building of the superb spacious clerestory of the choir.

Norwich's Norman castle-keep (left, 28177) is all that survives of the medieval castle buildings and is a remarkable structure. Built around 1100, on a low hill, it replaced an earlier Norman timber castle. At over 70 ft high it dominates many parts of the town. The old cattle market occupied part of the former bailey of the castle. In 1993 it was replaced by the very successful design of the Castle Mall shopping centre, partly built underground below a raised park.

Opposite:
NORWICH, THE CATHEDRAL AND PULL'S FERRY 1891 *28157p*

Above:
NORWICH, THE CATTLE MARKET AND THE CASTLE 1891 *28177*

Left:
NORWICH, ELM HILL 1929 *81806*

Right:
NORWICH, THE CATHEDRAL INTERIOR, THE NAVE LOOKING EAST 1891 *28147*

ROYAL SANDRINGHAM

Norfolk

A country gentleman's home, without any suggestion of the palace or citadel.

A 19TH-CENTURY guidebook describes Sandringham and the royal family in glowing terms: 'Seven miles from King's Lynn, Sandringham is the home of the late King Edward VII. The house is in modern Elizabethan style. Over the door is carved an inscription: "This house was built by Albert, Prince of Wales, and Alexandra his wife, in the year of our Lord 1870".'

On the Sandringham estates Albert, later to be known as King Edward, was the country gentleman, and as he walked in tweeds and gaiters over his fields, he was the typical East Anglian gentleman farmer. Six hundred acres were farmed. Queen Alexandra and her daughters took their share in this country life; their model dairy was noted 'for the perfection and daintiness of its arrangements and the excellence of its produce'.

The exquisite estate was purchased by Queen Victoria for the royal family in 1861. Within its 7,000 acres are the lands of seven parishes, and a profusion of deep woods, sandy heathland and broad grassy rides, which are the haunt of deer. The house was built a decade later in the Tudor style, a cumbersome confection of stone and red brick.

Under the neatly-trimmed ivy and bushes is the entrance lodge to Sandringham House and gardens (right, 38401), which were subsequently opened to the public in the early 1900s.

First and last, Sandringham is 'a country gentleman's home, without any suggestion of the palace or citadel'.

Opposite:
SANDRINGHAM,
THE HOUSE FROM THE
LAKE C1955 *S58029*

Above:
SANDRINGHAM,
THE ENTRANCE LODGE
1896 *38401*

Left:
SANDRINGHAM,
THE GARDENER'S COTTAGE
1927 *79758*

Right:
SANDRINGHAM,
THE HERBACEOUS BORDER
1927 *79760*

NEWMARKET

Suffolk

NEWMARKET is the world's capital of horse racing. The town's connection with the sport dates back to the time of Charles II, although it was not until the reign of Victoria that horse racing received its biggest boost, promoted by her son the Prince of Wales.

Stable lads exercising racehorses on Newmarket Heath is a daily sight around Newmarket. It is also common to see unsaddled horses being led along the centre of the High Street, as in N23033 below. Could they be going to a Tattersalls sale?

Below right:
NEWMARKET,
HIGH STREET
1929 81958

Above right:
NEWMARKET,
THE
RACECOURSE
C1960 N23066

Opposite:
NEWMARKET,
RACEHORSES
EXERCISING
C1955 N23033p

ITS races are said to have originated in the arrival of some horses which escaped the wreck of the Spanish armada; and they acquired celebrity by the erection here of a palatial hunting-seat of James I, called the King's House, which was rebuilt by Charles II. There are numerous stables belonging to trainers in the town and neighbourhood, the different training establishments affording accommodation to about 2,000 horses. The race-ground lies on the Downs, about a mile west of the town, and has a rich variety of arrangement and a pre-eminent degree of adaptation. The Beacon course, which is seldom used, being too severe for the horses, has a circuit of 4 miles, 1 furlong, 138 yards; the Round course, 3 miles, 4 furlongs, 167 yards; and ten other courses, less and various, the shortest being 2 furlongs, 47 yards. Races are run eight times in the year.

BRABNER'S GAZETTEER C1895

'AND laughs the immortal river still, Under the mill, under the mill'. So wrote the poet Rupert Brooke about Grantchester's mill. The river may well be immortal, but the mill certainly was not. It burned down in 1928.

The last two lines of Rupert Brooke's poem 'The Old Vicarage, Grantchester' have immortalised the village church: 'Stands the church clock at ten to three, And is there honey still for tea?' It is believed that the clock was actually broken when the poet was living in Grantchester. For years after Brooke's death in the First World War, the clock was kept at that time as a memorial to him.

The charming photograph of children walking along the path beside Byron's Pool (opposite top, 84546) shows a shaded woodland scene half a mile upstream on the river Cam from Grantchester. Undergraduates, including Byron, walked out from Cambridge to this pool for a dip in the summer.

In the view of the village street (opposite below, G44005), a thatcher is patching the long straw thatch of the cottage row; the nearer cottage butts against the former farmhouse, and has a pantiled roof with sloping dormer windows.

GRANTCHESTER
Cambridgeshire

THE OLD VICARAGE, GRANTCHESTER

JUST NOW the lilac is in bloom,
All before my little room;
And in my flower-beds, I think,
Smile the carnation and the pink;
And down the borders, well I know,
The poppy and the pansy blow . . .
Oh! there the chestnuts, summer through,
Beside the river make for you
A tunnel of green gloom, and sleep
Deeply above; and green and deep
The stream mysterious glides beneath,
Green as a dream and deep as death . . .

Ah God! to see the branches stir
Across the moon at Grantchester!
To smell the thrilling-sweet and rotten
Unforgettable, unforgotten
River-smell, and hear the breeze
Sobbing in the little trees.
Say, do the elm-clumps greatly stand
Still guardians of that holy land? . . .
And after, ere the night is born,
Do hares come out about the corn?
Oh, is the water sweet and cool,
Gentle and brown, above the pool?
And laughs the immortal river still
Under the mill, under the mill?
Say, is there Beauty yet to find?
And Certainty? and Quiet kind?
Deep meadows yet, for to forget
The lies, and truths, and pain? . . . oh! yet
Stands the church clock at ten to three?
And is there honey still for tea?

RUPERT BROOKE (1887–1915)

Opposite:
GRANTCHESTER, THE OLD MILL 1914 *66908a*

Above:
GRANTCHESTER, BYRON'S POOL C1931 *84546*

Left:
GRANTCHESTER, HIGH STREET C1955 *G44005*

LINCOLN
Lincolnshire

LINCOLN stands where the River Witham cuts through a ridge of limestone hills. Strategically positioned, the city had its own inland port – Brayford Pool – that connected it with the River Trent and the sea beyond.

The marvellously evocative late-Victorian view of the cathedral and Stonebow (right, 25654), taken from south of High Bridge, perfectly captures the essential character of Lincoln. The great medieval minster church dominates the city and the countryside for miles around. Many of the buildings that line the High Street have been rebuilt, some of them twice since 1890, while St Peter at Arches Church, whose Georgian tower peers over the rooftops, was demolished in 1933.

Left:
LINCOLN,
THE CATHEDRAL
AND STONEBOW
1890 *25654*

Below left:
LINCOLN,
CASTLE HILL 1906
55115a

Times have changed in all the country around; the wild fowl have departed from the fen, and the bittern's boom has been replaced by the hum of the threshing machine … but the three towers still look on, as man comes and man goes, as knowledge widens and phantoms are dispelled.

VICTORIAN GUIDEBOOK

LOOKING from in front of Exchequer Gate towards the castle the buildings on the right of the photograph are a splendid mix (left, 55115a): the jettied timber-framed Tudor building of about 1543 with its three gables contrasts with the early Georgian warm red brick houses beyond, and even more so with the austere and precise Judge's Lodgings of 1810 in pale stock brick. The Norman castle building involved the demolition of over 160 Anglo-Saxon houses. Since the Middle Ages the castle has served as a prison and assize courts. Much Norman stonework survives in the core of the present walls. Throughout the Middle Ages the town walls were patched, rebuilt and repaired, and ditches re-dug, only disappearing gradually after Tudor times; the gates, medieval and Roman, were mostly demolished in the 18th century.

The Jew's House (opposite below, 25664) is another of Lincoln's surviving early medieval stone houses: the city has more than most. It was a merchant's house with shops on the ground floor and the hall and chamber on the upper floor, the hall being heated by a stone fireplace above the doorway. To the left The Strait descends towards High Street. Now the headquarters of the Society for Lincolnshire History and Archaeology, the Jew's House dates from the 1170s and was indeed once owned by a Jewess, Belaset, in the 1280s. At the rear is Jew's Court where it is said Little St Hugh of Lincoln was crucified by Jews in 1255, although this story is given little credence by historians.

Above left:
LINCOLN,
THE GUILD HALL
1890 *25657t*

Above right:
LINCOLN,
STEEP HILL 1923
74640

Left:
LINCOLN,
THE JEW'S HOUSE
1890 *25664*

STEEP Hill (above, 74640) is a very famous narrow and, obviously, steep hill that has been much photographed over the years. It is rich in timber-framed buildings. This 1923 photograph shows people toiling uphill past Syson's with the timber-framed upper storey of Harding House Gallery on the right. This house was stone built to the lower floors and timber-framed to the third storey and has been much rebuilt. It is called Harding House because it was given to the city by a Canon Harding.

Stonebow is the city's celebrated 15th-century medieval gate. It was considerably added to and restored in the 1880s. In the photograph above left (25657t) we are looking towards the decorative archway.

CHESTER
Cheshire

FEW British cities have changed as little as Chester in the last 100 years. Saved from heavy industry by the silting up of the Dee, in the 19th century it was a quiet country town providing a prosperous farming county with facilities for business, lawsuits and entertainment.

The strategic importance of the site now occupied by Chester was realised by the Romans during their campaigns against the Brigantes and the Welsh. The site was on the north bank of the Dee at the lowest bridging point before the estuary.

In more recent times Chester was the first stop on the highly uncomfortable stagecoach route from Liverpool to London, used by those going to and from Ireland, which accounts for the city's large number of inns. Much of what we find most attractive about the Chester street scene today was built in the later decades of the 19th century. A few carefully-preserved houses of Tudor origin can still be seen, but most of the larger black-and-white buildings in Chester's main streets are such excellent imitations of the style that their lack of antiquity does not detract in any way from the pleasure they give to the visitor.

Of special delight are the covered walkways at first floor level, known as the Rows. Great care was taken during the Victorian reconstruction of the city centre to retain them; they continue to provide not only an additional layer of weatherproof shopping, but a wonderful vantage point from which to view the scene below.

The view on the right (46216) shows Eastgate, which was the entry point of the Roman road, the Via Devana. It was rebuilt as an elegant arch in 1769. The clock, made by J B Joyce of Whitchurch, was presented to the city by Edward Evans-Lloyd in 1897 to commemorate Queen Victoria's Diamond Jubilee.

Left:
CHESTER, EASTGATE STREET C1955 *C82060t*

Opposite:
CHESTER, EASTGATE 1900 *46216*

THIS area of the city is known as the Cross. In Roman times several roads met at this spot and, until it was demolished during the Civil War, a medieval cross stood nearby. The cross was restored to its original site in 1975. The origins of Watergate Row (opposite below, 1525) are debatable. This consists of continuous galleries above the ground-floor level giving access to other, totally separate, shops. They probably started to develop in the form that we see them today as early as the 13th century. It may well be that they echo a Roman pattern of domestic building – a combination of workshops and shops, the Roman equivalent of modern convenience shopping and residential apartments.

I LIKE this place much; but somehow I feel glad when I get among the quiet eighteenth-century buildings, in cosy places with some elbow room about them after the older architecture. This other is bedevilled and furtive; it seems to stoop; I am afraid of trap-doors, and could not go pleasantly into such houses. I don't know how much of this is legitimately the effect of the architecture; little enough possibly; possibly far the most part of it comes from bad historical novels and the disquieting statuary that garnishes some facades.

ROBERT LOUIS STEVENSON (1850–1894)

Opposite:
CHESTER, THE CROSS 1903 *49881*

Below:
CHESTER, WATERGATE ROW 1863 *1525*

Right:
CHESTER, WATERGATE STREET 1888 *20608*

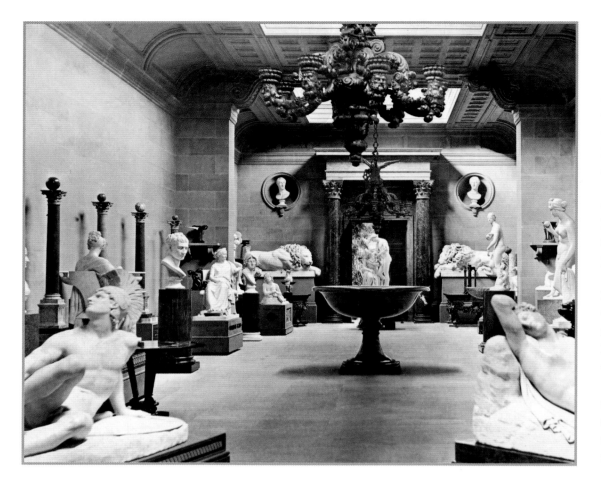

CHATSWORTH HOUSE, the magnificent stately home of the Dukes of Devonshire, and often called the 'Palace of the Peak', is situated near Rowsley, and is one of the beauties of Derbyshire. The old hall was reconstructed partly by Sir William Cavendish, and partly by his widow Bess of Hardwick. Mary Queen of Scots was kept prisoner in the old house. Built between 1687 and 1706, with the north wing added in 1820, Chatsworth remains a veritable treasure house.

Opposite (18642) is the classic prospect of Chatsworth, the Palladian west front of Chatsworth House seen from James Paine's entrance bridge over the River Derwent. The only change that modern visitors to Derbyshire's most popular stately home will note is that the classical statues on the bridge piers are no longer present.

The gardens were almost exclusively the work of Joseph Paxton, the Duke of Devonshire's gardener and architectural genius, who went on to design London's Crystal Palace. In the photograph below left (8848), we see the Egyptian statue of Sekhmet (left), which is now in the house in the Chapel Passage, and the 1st Duke's greenhouse, the Camellia House, on the right with its classic Georgian windows.

The Sculpture Gallery at Chatsworth (above left, 8853) illustrates very well the quality of the fabulous art collection which successive Dukes of Devonshire have acquired over the years. Here classical marble sculptures line the walls and floor, to be shared with the thousands of visitors who annually come to 'the Palace of the Peak'.

Above left:
CHATSWORTH HOUSE,
THE SCULPTURE HALL c1876
8853

Below left:
CHATSWORTH HOUSE,
THE GARDENS c1876 *8848*

Left:
CHATSWORTH HOUSE, CUPID
IN THOUGHT c1876 *8859*

Opposite:
CHATSWORTH HOUSE AND
THE BRIDGE 1886 *18642*

CHATSWORTH HOUSE

Derbyshire

Chatsworth has always appeared to us an unsatisfactory place. The house is not situated on a platform of adequate size, and there is awkwardness in the approach proceeding abruptly up the hill. A square pile of a building, too, in such a situation, is less suitable than a lengthened one ... The improvements now going on will probably remedy most of the evils. The house is being extended in length; and the approach may be made by a bridge across the river.

JOHN CLAUDIUS LOUDON 1831

DERBYSHIRE DALES

Derbyshire

THE Derbyshire Dales is one of these very special landscapes - an area instantly identifiable by its spectacular, crag-bound and wooded limestone dales dissecting the relatively flat but gently rolling 1,000ft-high plateau. In most cases, and in sharp contrast to their counterparts in Yorkshire, the Derbyshire Dales are too narrow and precipitous to accommodate a road. So the only way properly to explore the quiet, sylvan beauty of the Derbyshire Dales is on foot, and we may be thankful that they are blessed with some of the most beautiful riverside footpaths in Britain.

The delights of the dales as a place to visit have been extolled over the years ever since Lord Byron enquired of his friend the Irish poet Thomas Moore: 'Was you ever in Dovedale? I assure you there are things in Derbyshire as noble as in Greece or Switzerland'.

THE river is a shallow, sparkling stream, with many a pool dear to the angler, and hurrying down, babbling over pebbles, and broken in its course by many a tiny waterfall. On both sides rise tall limestone cliffs, splintered into countless fantastic forms – rocky walls, towers, and pinnacles, and in one place a natural archway near the summit, leading to the uplands beyond. And all up the sloping sides, and wherever root-hold could be obtained on pinnacle and crag, were clustered shrubs and trees of every shade of foliage, with the first touch of autumn to heighten the exquisite variety by tints which as yet suggested only afar off the thought of decay. The solitude of the scene served but to enhance its loveliness.

THE REVEREND SAMUEL MANNING c1885

Below left:
DOVEDALE,
THE STEPPING
STONES 1914 *67609*

Above:
GOYT VALLEY 1914
67584

Right:
BUXTON, THE CAT &
FIDDLE 1914 *67581p*

Opposite above:
MATLOCK BATH
c1864 *2096*

Opposite below:
HADDON HALL
c1870 *5232*

Was you ever in Dovedale? I assure you there are things in Derbyshire as noble as in Greece or Switzerland. LORD BYRON (1788–1824)

THE Dove (opposite below, 67609), was famous in Victorian times for its fishing. Here we see children crossing the stepping stones. A little further on a footbridge led to the Isaac Walton Hotel, where rooms costs from 3s 6d and lunch or dinner from 2s 6d.

The Goyt (opposite above, 67584) was one of the excursions available to tourists visiting Buxton. Here, several groups have stopped to enjoy lunch.

The Cat & Fiddle (below, 67581p), on the lonely road from Buxton to Macclesfield, was and still is the highest inn in England. The building has been enlarged since this photograph was taken.

Often described as the most perfect medieval manor house in England, Haddon Hall (below right, 5232), has been the Derbyshire home of the Dukes of Rutland for many generations. A formally-dressed Victorian group pose decorously in the porch of the entrance to the banqueting hall. Note the Vernon and Manners crests carved above the doorway, and the neatly-trimmed box hedges on the right.

Known as 'Little Switzerland' to generations of tourists, Matlock Bath (right, 2096) has long attracted visitors to its craggy limestone gorge cut by the River Derwent. This view looks down on the hillside villas from the road which winds up to the Temple Hotel.

SALTAIRE is on the Midland Railway main line from Bradford to Skipton. In the background to this view of the station is Titus Salt's pioneering mill and community. Salt moved his alpaca and mohair mills here in the 1850s. The mill was six storeys high, its weaving shed held 1,200 looms, and there was a workforce of over 3,000. Visitors to Saltaire were not just treated to an industrial centre. On the outskirts of Saltaire lies a beautiful glen, which in Victorian times was a firm favourite for a summer-time walk. High above here an amusement park was established with an aerial ride, Japanese gardens and a switchback railway. A toboggan ride also careered down the side of the glen, but it was closed in 1900 after an accident. The Glen Tramway is a delightful way to travel to the top – it has been operating for over a century.

SALTAIRE

West Yorkshire

THIS area was built by the mill owner Titus Salt as a model industrial village alongside a canal, river and railway, well away from the pollution of Bradford. Provision was made for welfare benefits and help was given to the aged, infirm and sick. The Club and Institute, now the Victoria Hall, provided enlightenment and education for the workers and their children. Outside the hall are four sculptured lions, made for Trafalgar Square, but considered too small. Only two things were excluded from this village – a pub and a pawn shop.

Titus Salt's Victorian idealism led him to believe that a happy, healthy and fulfilled workforce was a productive workforce. His model village provided all the essential living amenities, and for recreation he provided a spacious park on the opposite side of the river and canal. Here splendid gardens, with statues of Salt, offered healthy living to the workers at the giant mill. The park was later called Roberts Park, after being bought by another industrialist, and was then offered to Bradford Council.

Opposite: SALTAIRE, THE STATION 1909 *61871*

Above left: SALTAIRE, THE MILL AND THE CRICKET PITCH 1888 *21024*

Below left: SALTAIRE, ROBERTS PARK 1909 *61872*

HE has reared up a palace to labour!
Will equal the Cæsars of old;
The Church and the School and the Cottage,
And lavished his thousands in gold;
Where the workman may live and be happy,
Enjoying the fruit of his hand,
In contentment, and comfort, and plenty,
Secure as a peer of the land.

Then let us all join in the chorus,
And sing of the qualities rare,
Of one who by nature is noble,
And hail him the Lord of Saltaire!

HOLROYD, 'THE LORD OF SALTAIRE'

BRONTË COUNTRY

Yorkshire

HAWORTH is a small town of cobbled streets and plain grey stone houses set amidst the moors near Keighley. In the parsonage here were born the Brontë sisters, Emily, Charlotte and Anne, and their brother Bramwell. Their father was the vicar of St Michael and All Angels' Church. The moors around were beautiful but bleak, and the sisters led often solitary lives. The wild landscapes surely gave them the inspiration for their novels.

The Parsonage (below, H194023) was built in the late 1700s from locally quarried millstone grit. It stood opposite the churchyard and was continually battered by the fierce winds off the high moors.

Top Withens (opposite, H194045) is an isolated farmhouse high up on the bleak wastes of Haworth Moor. Historians say that Emily Brontë used it as the site for Wuthering Heights. However, she must have employed considerable poetic licence, because it bears no resemblance to the house in which the Earnshaws lived.

Below right (79108) is the house at Cowan Bridge where Charlotte Brontë and her sisters attended the Clergy Daughter's School. Their unhappy experience here, which resulted in the deaths of Maria and Elizabeth Brontë from consumption, is believed to be the basis for Lowood School in 'Jane Eyre'.

Left:
HAWORTH, BRONTË BRIDGE C1955 H194036

Below left:
HAWORTH, THE PARSONAGE C1955 H194023

Below right:
COWAN BRIDGE, WHERE CHARLOTTE BRONTË WENT TO SCHOOL 1926 79108

Opposite:
TOP WITHENS, 'WUTHERING HEIGHTS' C1955 H194045

WUTHERING Heights is the name of Mr Heathcliff's dwelling. 'Wuthering' being a significant provincial adjective, descriptive of the atmospheric tumult to which its station is exposed in stormy weather. Pure, bracing ventilation they must have up there at all times, indeed; one may guess the power of the north wind blowing over the edge, by the excessive slant of a few stunted firs at the end of the house; and by a range of gaunt thorns all stretching their limbs one way, as if craving alms of the sun. Happily, the architect had foresight to build it strong: the narrow windows are deeply set in the walls, and the corners defended with large jutting stones.

EMILY BRONTË, 'WUTHERING HEIGHTS' 1847

FOUNTAINS ABBEY

Yorkshire

VISITORS to Ripon could hire a carriage to take them on the six-mile round trip to Fountains Abbey, or, if they were feeling up to it, they could enjoy a promenade through the woods to reach it.

This glorious Cistercian abbey, now a delightful medley of lichen-covered ruins, was founded in poverty in 1132, and building work continued to 1524. It was given large tracts of land on which to raise sheep. A huge amount of English wool was sold abroad, often by means of forward contracts, which enabled the monks to spend money on ever more grand buildings. At one time, Fountains had over 600,000 acres of land given over to wool production. The Studley Royal Estate close by has exquisite gardens laid out by William Aislabie. He acquired the abbey ruins in 1767 and landscaped the grounds.

Left:
STUDLEY ROYAL,
THE WATER GARDEN
c1880 *7391*

Right:
FOUNTAINS ABBEY
1886 *18352*

The grassy meadow by the rippling stream, the thickly wooded slopes, the ivy grown crags of cream-coloured limestone, can have changed but little in all these 750 years. TOURIST GUIDE 1890

THE WOODED APPROACH TO FOUNTAINS

PRESENTLY the signs of the landscape art of Studley Royal are less conspicuous; the valley slightly narrows, and becomes more abrupt and rocky; we emerge from the woods on a level grassy meadow, at the end of which stand the grey ruins of the abbey. These, though the hand of man has been plain in the trim pleasaunces of Studley, startle us even now, not only by the sudden change from present to past, but still more by the apparition of so great a pile in the lonely uplands. The buildings extend completely across the bed of the valley – on the right hand there is only room for a road between the transept of the church and the limestone crags, and the stones in its stately tower seem to be almost brushed by the branches of the trees rooted in the crannies of the rock.

TOURIST GUIDE 1890

THE YORKSHIRE DALES

Yorkshire

THERE are few scenes more instantly identifiable as English than the typical view of one of the Yorkshire Dales, with picturesque stone villages in the deep valleys and the broad moorland heights stretching across the horizon above. Some of the country's finest limestone and gritstone scenery make up the 638-square mile (1,769-sq km) Yorkshire Dales National Park – Britain's third largest after the Lake District and Snowdonia. Today's National Park, which was designated in 1954 and receives more than nine million annual visits, is, however, largely the creation of man, as the stone-walled fields and barns of the dales show.

It was in the Middle Ages that farming developed into a truly sustainable economy in the Dales. Vast sheep ranches and granges were established by the land-hungry monks of the great religious houses, such as those at Bolton Abbey in Wharfedale and Jervaulx in Wensleydale. The white-robed Cistercian monks gloried in their poverty, but paradoxically they were also great and highly successful entrepreneurs, and were among the first to build mills to harness the abundant water power of Dales rivers.

With the first railways which threaded the Dales – such as the 72-mile Settle to Carlisle railway built between 1869 and 1876 – came the first tourists, to gape in wonder at attractions such as the Ingleton Glens, Kilnsey Crag and Malham Cove.

Granted a market charter in 1699 by William III, Hawes (above right, 60795) later became a centre for textiles, quarrying and the production of Wensleydale cheese. The outdoor market is still held on a Tuesday, though a Market Hall was opened in 1902. In 1887, an auction mart was established for the sale of livestock; before this, auctions were held in the main street. The parish church of St Margaret was rebuilt in the mid 19th century at a cost of around £3,000, having originally been erected in the late 15th century.

Mechanisation might well have reached market traders, but down on the farm things were different. In the picture opposite (75754), a sled is being put to good use during haymaking near Hawes.

Two labourers pose for the camera at Addleborough (below right, 67235). They have been scything, and are probably travelling between fields. Addleborough peak in the background is believed to have been named after a British chieftain, Authulf.

Opposite:
HAWES, HAYMAKING 1924   *75754t*

Above right:
HAWES, MARKET DAY 1908   *60795*

Below right:
ADDLEBOROUGH, FARM WORKERS 1914   *67235*

Wooded slopes and grassy banks, grey lines of crags, with wild moorlands rising on either hand rising above the richer scenery of the more sheltered dale . VICTORIAN GUIDEBOOK

REDMIRE (left, 82588) lies three miles west of Leyburn. Lead mining was a major employer here, as was stone quarrying, but these industries have since declined, leaving Redmire in peaceful seclusion. The stone pillar we see here was erected in 1887, and the village was supplied with lamps to commemorate the 50th year of Queen Victoria's reign. An electric lamp was fitted to the top of the pillar in 1977 to mark the Silver Jubilee of Elizabeth II's reign.

Leyburn, (below left, 21690), at the eastern end of Wensleydale, boasts no fewer than three squares, the largest being the sloping rectangular Market Place which can be seen in the distance in this view from the tower of the village church. A weekly market is still held here on a Friday, as it has been since its charter was granted in 1686.

Bainbridge, (below, 82600), stands astride the River Bane, which at just three miles in length is said to be the shortest river in England. It flows from Semerwater, which with a surface area of about ninety acres was the largest lake in the North Riding, to the River Ure. Bainbridge was once an important crossroads where roads from Lancaster, Swaledale, and Westmoreland met; it was also a settlement for woodsmen working in the great forest of Wensleydale.

Above: REDMIRE, THE VILLAGE 1929 *82588*

Below left: LEYBURN, MARKET PLACE 1889 *21690*

Below right: BAINBRIDGE, THE GREEN 1929 *82600*

Opposite left: RICHMOND, THE CASTLE KEEP 1908 *59493t*

Opposite right: RICHMOND, CASTLE AND BRIDGE 1893 *32275*

IN photograph 32275 (above) we are looking past John Carr's Green Bridge towards Richmond's magnificent castle – a true picture of medieval England. The castle was built from 1071 by Alan the Red as a defence station at the gateway to Swaledale. Although the castle has never experienced a siege, it has remained a military base. The first recorded market took place at Richmond in 1155; by 1440 the town was trading in a variety of commodities, ranging from dairy produce, wine and fish, to coal, lead-ore, copper and silk.

THE situation of Richmond is one of singular beauty, and the ruins are of exceptional interest. The town is perched on the summit of a plateau … The river takes a bold curving sweep, so that nature has carved out of the plateau a bastion-like headland … From the market place a narrow and crooked street leads to the entrance of the castle. This noble remnant has suffered singularly little from the assaults of man or time; 'stern and massive', and with scarce a tuft of vegetation along its ledges, it has not been 'mouldered into beauty', but still frowns with all its battlements almost as when it passed from the hands of Conan's masons.

VICTORIAN GUIDEBOOK

A POLICEMAN directs the traffic in Parliament Street (above, 74570). On the right are the Royal Baths, which cost nearly £100,000 to build; even the Kursaal, which opened in 1903, cost over £70,000. The money lavished on providing Harrogate with the best spa facilities in the country ensured that the town remained the most fashionable of all the spas for 50 years.

The stagecoaches in the photograph of the Stray (left, 48067) are probably being used on excursions. In the background the buildings are Montpelier Parade (left), Cambridge Crescent (centre), and the Prospect Hotel which opened in 1859, but was enlarged in 1870. At this time, a room at the Prospect cost from 4s 6d per day; dinner cost 6s. It is hard to believe that Smollett could have described prosperous Harrogate in such unprepossessing terms as he did:

A wild common, bare and bleak, without tree or shrub, or the least sign of cultivation

TOBIAS SMOLLETT (1721–1771)

HARROGATE
Yorkshire

HARROGATE is one of the oldest and most loved of the English spa towns. The discovery of spa water in 1571 by Sir William Slingsby led to a remarkable period in the town's history. In Low Harrogate hotels and stylish crescents were built, attracting a very high-class visitor.

The Pump Room (left, 48974) was constructed in 1842 over the sulphur wells. Now it is a fascinating museum, where visitors are encouraged to sample the health-giving water. To the left is Hales Bar, a coaching inn from 1849, and behind the Pump Room is the Crown Hotel, rebuilt in 1847.

Valley Gardens (below left, 58645) was a favourite place for a mild constitutional after taking the waters. Here a small crowd enjoys an afternoon concert given by a pierrot troupe.

The spa trade declined in the 1920s – although more visitors came, they spent less money. The fashion for health spas was on the wane. But before the Great War, times were still genteel, and enjoyment came from simple pleasures.

BY seven o'clock it is time to be stirring, and from that till the breakfast hour there is a stream – not only of halt and lame, but also of hale and hearty visitors – to the old Royal and new Royal Baths Pump Rooms, where 'bumpers' of sulphuric and chalybeate waters are dispensed at a charge of 6d a day. After the first glass a mild constitutional is recommended, and this is usually taken up the prettily laid-out Valley Gardens. We write from little personal experience of the properties of these waters, or of the rotation in which they should be taken, but we are told that a quarter-of-an-hour after the strong, a dose of the mild sulphur is the rule, and apart from their hygienic qualities, we believe it is quite possible to acquire a taste for these rotten egg and at first extremely unpalatable refreshers, especially as they are served up warm.

VICTORIAN GUIDEBOOK

YORK

Yorkshire

THE walled city of York was for centuries the second most important city in England. Fortified by the Romans, it was here in AD 306 that Constantine the Great was proclaimed emperor. The historical and cultural capital of northern England, York has managed to survive the ravages of time, and is still able to offer visitors a fascinating glimpse into its 2,000 years of history.

The Victorians loved York, and travellers came from all over to enjoy its splendours, arriving by stage and mail-coach. There was also a steamboat service to and from London. The coming of the railways put York firmly on the tourist map. Though the lines were owned by the North Eastern, no fewer than five other companies ran trains into the city – underlining York's importance as a regional railway centre. For decades, the first indication for those travelling by train that York was just a few miles away was the sight of the lofty towers of the Minster rising majestically above the city roofs.

No part of the Minster is better worthy of admiration than that which strikes the eye as we approach from the station – the West Front, Decorated, and unequalled in its style in the kingdom. VICTORIAN GUIDEBOOK

THE present York Minster is not the first place of worship to be built on the site. It is believed that there was first a wooden church, then one of stone, which were followed by three other churches. Some of these were destroyed by fire: the worst blaze was in 1137, which not only raged through the church but also destroyed a large portion of the town, including St Mary's Abbey and another 39 churches.

Begun by Archbishop Walter de Gray during the reign of King John and finally completed in July 1472, the present minster stands on a site previously occupied by the Roman praetorium and Saxon churches; the earliest of these was a small wattle oratory constructed for the baptism of Edwin, King of Northumbria, during the Easter celebrations of 627. The minster is one of the largest cathedrals in England at over 546 ft in length and 222 ft across the transepts. The western towers are 196 ft high, whilst the central tower rises over 100 ft above the intersection of the nave, choir, and transepts.

The stained glass in York is considered to be among the finest in the world. The glass that survives in the minster and the medieval churches was often donated in memory of someone after a bereavement, or as a gift, by wealthy families who were parishioners of that particular church.

To the right of view 59785 (above) is Duncombe Place, with the tall memorial to the soldiers who took part in the Boer War. It was erected in 1905.

Opposite:
YORK, THE MINSTER 1908 *59785*

Above:
YORK, LOW PETERGATE 1892 *30632*

THIS narrow, twisting street with its fine old jettied houses was originally part of the Roman fort's main road, or *Via Principalis*. On the right are the premises of Merriman the pawnbroker, with its leaf-decorated lamp hanging above the shop front. On the left is a large sweeping brush head trade sign, now in the York Castle Museum: it advertised Seale's Brush and Mat Warehouse. The lamp on the front of the Londesbro Arms has now disappeared. This photograph perfectly conjures the atmosphere of medieval York.

IN the view of Goodramgate (right, 30631) we see Victorian street advertising at its best. Websters, on the extreme left, are offering to sole and heel men's boots for 2s 6d a pair; women's boots are somewhat cheaper at 1s 6d a pair. John Wharton – we believe that is him standing in the doorway – owned the Cheap Shop, an early discount store offering china, glassware, lamps, brushes, wicks, lamp oil and so on at competitive prices. The covered way at the side of J Todd the grocer and tea dealer's was built for the vicars-choral, so that they could cross from where they lived in Bedern to the Minster Yard without being molested. The grocer's became an office for the National Trust in 1903. It was situated where College Street joins Goodramgate on the eastern side.

The word Shambles derives from 'shamel', meaning benches or stalls. In the 15th century, this little street (opposite, 61722) was full of open-fronted butchers' stalls with the meat being displayed hanging from large hooks. Up to the 19th century there were still many butchers selling their meat here.

The archway to Bootham Bar (right, 63585) dates from the 11th century; this is the oldest of York's gates. In medieval times, guards were posted to keep watch and to guide people from the nearby Forest of Galtres so as to protect them from the packs of wolves that roamed the area.

Opposite: YORK, THE SHAMBLES 1909 *61722*

Above right: YORK, GOODRAMGATE 1892 *30631t*

Below right: YORK, BOOTHAM BAR 1911 *63585*

Below: YORK, BOOTHAM BAR AND THE MINSTER 1893 *32032*

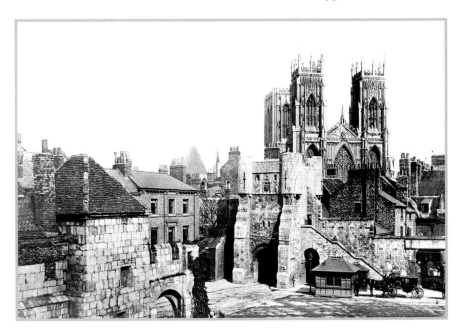

DATING back to Roman times, this is the only natural harbour between the Humber and the Tees, and so it is an important shipping haven. For centuries the people of Whitby earned their living from the sea. St Mary's Church and the ruins of Whitby Abbey stand on the hill overlooking the harbour. We are looking towards the East Cliff, where the old parish church of St Mary and the ruins of Whitby Abbey stand. St Mary's is 12th-century, consisting of a nave, chancel, and tower. Though the exterior is plain, the interior is one of the most outstanding in England. There are galleries on every side; box pews date back to the 17th century; there is a three-decker pulpit of 1778; and all is lit by candlelight. The church was made famous by Bram Stoker in his Gothic novel 'Dracula' as the place where the count sought refuge in the grave of a suicide.

THE houses of the old town – the side away from us, are all red-roofed, and seem piled up one over the other anyhow, like the pictures we see of Nuremberg. Right over the town is the ruin of Whitby Abbey, which was sacked by the Danes, and which is the scene of part of 'Marmion', where the girl was built up in the wall. It is a most noble ruin, of immense size, and full of beautiful and romantic bits. There is a legend that a white lady is seen in one of the windows. Between it and the town there is another church, the parish one, round which is a big graveyard, all full of tombstones. This is to my mind the nicest spot in Whitby, for it lies right over the town, and has a full view of the harbour and all up the bay to where the headland called Kettleness stretches out into the sea. It descends so steeply over the harbour that part of the bank has fallen away, and some of the graves have been destroyed … The harbour lies below me, with, on the far side, one long granite wall stretching out into the sea, with a curve outwards at the end of it, in the middle of which is a lighthouse … I shall come and sit here often myself and work. Indeed, I am writing now, with my book on my knee, and listening to the talk of three old men who are sitting beside me. They seem to do nothing all day but sit here and talk.

BRAM STOKER 'DRACULA' 1897

WHITBY
Yorkshire

Opposite:
WHITBY, EAST CLIFF
1913 *66263*

Right:
WHITBY, TIN GHAUT
1913 *66292*

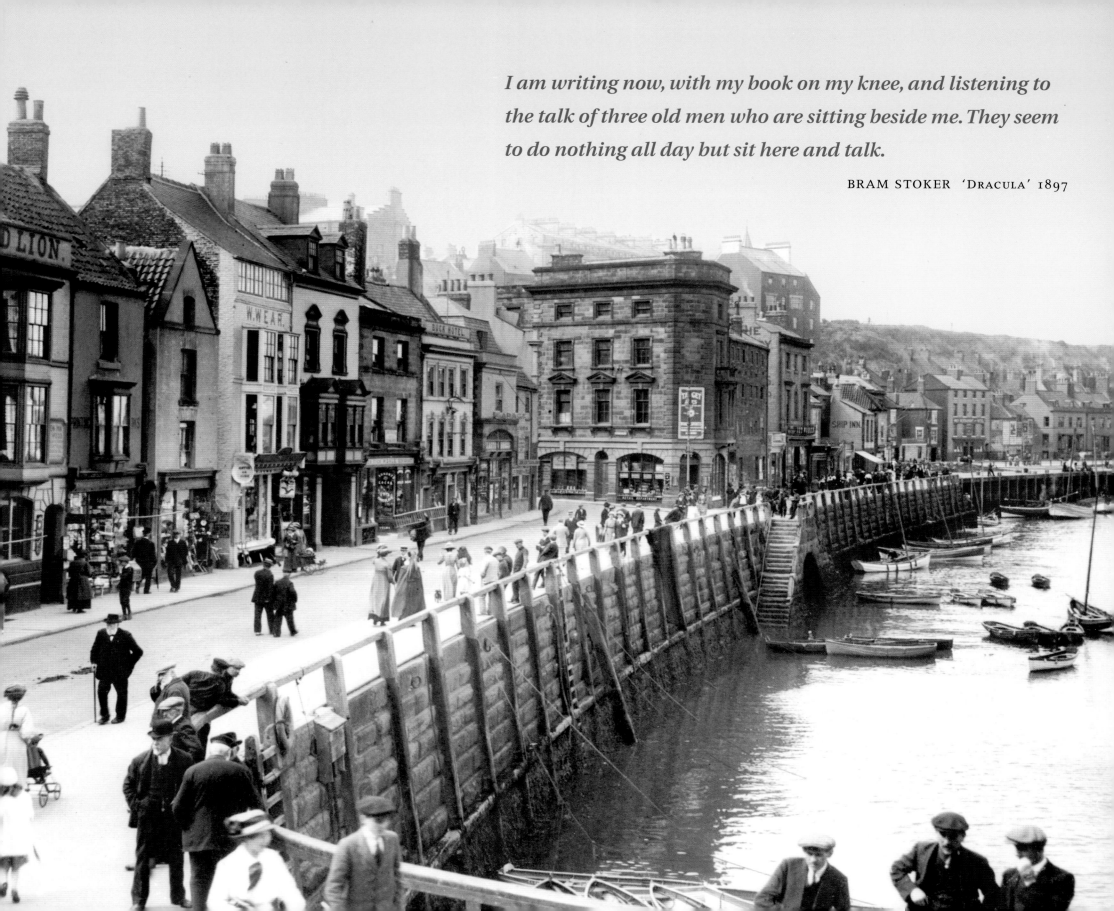

I am writing now, with my book on my knee, and listening to the talk of three old men who are sitting beside me. They seem to do nothing all day but sit here and talk.

BRAM STOKER 'DRACULA' 1897

LINKING the east and west sides of the town over the River Esk, the bridge (just visible in the foreground of the photograph opposite (66267) is now crammed with tourists in the summer months. Captain Cook was apprenticed here at the age of 17; there are many monuments to him here, including a statue and the Captain Cook Museum.

The town was once a whaling port, and there were blubber houses along the inner harbour. Whaling ships once departed from here to sail to the Arctic in search of a catch. Between 1766 and 1816 the local whaling fleet caught 2761 whales and about 25,000 seals. When whaling declined, herring became important to the town's prosperity; but the herring fishery is now all but gone, and the town relies mainly on tourism. Below right (74318) we see the fish market, packed with fishermen, dealers and visitors. A new fish market now exists on the harbourside, but little else is changed.

The coming of the railway put Whitby on the tourist map; its harbourside streets, ruined abbey, and souvenirs made from jet, which is a fossilized wood found locally, all proved a magnet for holidaymakers. Holiday trade led to much of the development in the town, chiefly in the direction of the West Cliff.

Opposite:
WHITBY, ST ANN'S STAITH 1913
66267t

Above right:
WHITBY, WATCHING THE FISHING
FLEET C1955 *W81148*

Below right:
WHITBY, THE FISH QUAY 1923 *74318*

Below:
WHITBY, 'GEMINI' 1891 *28862p*

THE MANCHESTER
SHIP CANAL

THE canal did not open until 1 January 1894. 36 miles long, and many years (and financial crises) under construction, it linked Manchester to the sea, allowing ocean-going ships to trade right into the city.

Below (M340501), two steamers head for the tidal lock at Eastham on their way out of the canal. On the right is the river Mersey, and to the left, by the building with a tall chimney, is the entrance to the Shropshire Union Canal. This area, partially redeveloped, is now home to the Boat Museum.

The photograph right (M21503) looks along the length of No 9 Dock towards No 2 Grain Elevator. The withdrawal of container traffic spelled the end for Manchester, and by the early 1980s the docks had been flattened in readiness for residential and leisure redevelopment.

Opposite far left: THE MANCHESTER SHIP CANAL, ELLESMERE PORT 1947 *M340501*

Opposite above: MANCHESTER, NO 9 DOCK C1965 *M21503*

Opposite below: BARTON-UPON-IRWELL, THE BARTON AQUEDUCT 1894 *33693*

Above: BARTON-UPON-IRWELL, THE SWING BRIDGES 1895 *33691*

THIS view shows the two bridges at Barton-upon-Irwell both swung aside to let the paddle steamer 'Ivanhoe' pass. When the Ship Canal first opened (our view is only 12 months after that opening on 1 January 1894), many people wanted to travel, and see the wonders of this new waterway. A Ship Canal Pleasure Steamer Company was formed, and weekends and Bank Holidays would see two or three of these paddle steamers taking passengers on sight-seeing trips up and down the canal. Cargo ships would have tugs fore and aft to guide them through this section of the canal. Barton Monastery stands just to the right of the swing bridges; it was formerly All Saints' Roman Catholic Church, Barton. The area behind the bridges was the wood seasoning area for one of the large timber firms using the canal, and is now a housing estate.

THE area from the Duke of Wellington statue to Market Street was once a large ornamental pond complete with fountains, which had delighted Queen Victoria and Prince Albert on their visit in 1840. Before that, the area was called the 'dawb holes'; clay was taken from here to make local bricks. At the time of our picture (above, 22158), Piccadilly was newly laid out and paved. The cabs in the picture include the famous hansom cab, designed and built by Charles Hansom of Manchester.

The Royal Infirmary, with its high dome and clock face, lords it over Piccadilly. The hospital opened in 1775; the portico entrance facing the square was the front of a Mental Asylum, which was incorporated into the building. A public bath house was also part of the block; as well as serving the people of the back streets around Piccadilly, it meant that patients could be given a bath before entering hospital. On Tuesday 1 September 1908, a large crowd gathered here to watch about one hundred patients being moved out of the Infirmary. Horse-drawn ambulances, taxi cabs, flat wagons, and even a horse bus were used to convey the patients down to the new Royal Infirmary on Oxford Road. Only one patient was left behind because he was too ill to move. The main buildings were demolished, but the Wash House remained, as did part of the Asylum, which was used as a reference library.

MANCHESTER

Greater Manchester

'THE fastest growing town in England', was how Manchester was described two hundred and fifty years ago.

It gained a reputation as the business centre for the Lancashire cotton industry, and as the place where the first canal system was started, passenger railways were born, and plans for a great ship canal were hatched.

The town's progress to the status of city was rapid, probably the fastest in England. By 1839 it had its own Justice of the Peace, and by 1842 a coat of arms, a crest and motto – 'Concilio et Labore', 'By Council and Work'.

The Royal Exchange, with its dome and towers, dominates Exchange Street (left, 8290), which starts where the square becomes narrower. The statue of John Cobden can been seen in the middle of the square: this bronze statue, by Marshall Wood, was paid for by public subscription and was presented to the town on 23 April 1867 by the President of the Anti-Corn Law League, George Wilson.

The Exchange (below, 18262) was dubbed at the time 'the largest room in the world'. It was 4,405 square yards in area, and 96ft high and 125ft high to the top of the central dome. In this huge hall, cotton merchants from all over Lancashire did their bartering, and many a fortune was made or lost. At one stage there were eleven thousand members, who met every Tuesday and Friday to conduct business – 'each man intent on buying and selling, and helping to fill the room with a deep hum of voices like a gigantic beehive … Transaction of enormous magnitude are concluded in a few minutes' time' (from a Victorian guidebook).

Opposite:
MANCHESTER,
PICCADILLY 1889
22158

Above:
MANCHESTER,
ST ANN'S SQUARE
C1876 *8290*

Right:
MANCHESTER,
THE GREAT HALL,
THE ROYAL EXCHANGE
1885 *18262*

Each man [is] intent on buying and selling, and helping to fill the room with a deep hum of voices like a gigantic beehive … Transactions of enormous magnitude are concluded in a few minutes' time.

VICTORIAN GUIDEBOOK

LIVERPOOL
Merseyside

'GATEWAY to the British Empire', 'Second City in England', 'Door to the New World'. All these titles have been used to describe the city of Liverpool. 200 years ago it was a creek in the river; at the start of the 1900s Liverpool had built itself up into a world-class city with seven miles of docks full of ocean-going ships.

By the 1890s Liverpool would have had upwards of 200 ships every week leaving for every corner of the great British Empire, and indeed the world. Ships went to Canada for corn, and carried iron goods to South America and Africa.

As the 19th century drew to a close, Liverpool was an exciting, vibrant city. Its citizens forged ahead with great building projects and modernisation. They electrified the Mersey Underground Railway, and they built an overhead railway to connect the ever-expanding dock area. Shipping companies built citadels that matched their world status.

Over the years, the great liners have gone, and the river front is quiet. Containerisation, mechanisation, in fact a whole new world is now taking over; but instead of going into a decline, Liverpool is once more thriving in a different way, and rising to new challenges that lie ahead. Liverpool today is one of the country's most successful and promising cities.

The Mersey was gay and almost crowded with vessels of all sorts moving up and down the river ... THE REV FRANCIS KILVERT

THE Mersey was gay and almost crowded with vessels of all sorts moving up and down the river, ships, barques, brigs, brigantines, schooners, cutters, colliers, tugs, steamboats, lighters, 'flats', everything from the huge emigrant liner steamship with four masts to the tiny sailing and rowing boat. From the river one sees to advantage the miles of docks which line the Mersey side, and the forests of masts which crowd the quays, 'the pine forest of the sea, mast and spar' … Nothing gives one so vivid an idea of the vast commerce of the country as these docks, quays and immense warehouses, piled and cumbered with hides, cotton, tallow, corn, oilcake, wood and wine, oranges and other fruit and merchandise of all kinds from all corners of the world.
THE REVEREND FRANCIS KILVERT 1872

THE junction of Castle Street and Water Street, outside the Town Hall (left, 36650), has always been one of the busiest in Liverpool, and a natural meeting place. The balcony within the portico has seen some of the city's most memorable moments. Liverpool Football Club and Bill Shankly (and Everton as well in the 1930s) have waved to the crowds from here. The Beatles stood there in the late 1960s with a cheering crowd of 100,000 in Castle Street.

The building in photograph 36655 (below) was known as Exchange Flags when it first opened at the end of the 1700s. The Exchange building seen here was the third on this site; it was designed by T H Wyatt, and built in 1863. At one time you had to be invited to walk on the Exchange Flags. Much of the shipping and insurance business of the port was carried out in this square behind the Town Hall. In the middle of the Flags stands Nelson's monument, erected to the great man in 1813. It was Liverpool's first public monument, and was designed by Matthew Cotes Wyatt. The monument has four grilles which provide air vents for the tobacco warehouse that was once underneath it. Also under part of the Flags is the secret war-time bunker where the operations for the north Atlantic were master-minded.

The magnificent St George's Hall dominates the left side of the photograph of Lime Street (opposite, 26661). St George's Hall is unique, being a combination of two law courts, a concert hall, a theatre, a jail and cells. It is considered to be one of the finest buildings in the whole of Great Britain. The horse trams in the foreground would run for another decade before electric trams took their place. The Wellington column can be seen on the right-hand side of the picture.

Above: LIVERPOOL, THE TOWN HALL 1895 *36650*

Right: LIVERPOOL, THE EXCHANGE 1895 *36655*

Opposite: LIVERPOOL, LIME STREET 1890 *26661*

On one occasion the mayor and corporation, honest hospitable souls, were entertaining Prince William of Gloucester (who commanded the troops) at a banquet, and were so much delighted by his appetite that one of them exclaimed, 'Eat away, your Royal Highness, there's plenty more in the kitchen!'

VICTORIAN GUIDEBOOK

DURING the 1830s Blackpool was still developing along genteel lines, though for several decades the tradition of the Lancashire working people and their families visiting the town had already begun. With the coming of Bank Holidays and the railway, the resort started to boom. The North Pier opened in 1863, electric lighting was introduced along the promenade in 1879, and the first illuminated tramcars ran as early as 1897. The town tried to retain its sophisticated reputation, but the writing was on the wall in 1879, when the Winter Gardens' main attraction was a young lady being fired from a cannon!

In 1894 Blackpool pulled off the seaside coup of the century with the opening of the Blackpool Tower. Based on the Eiffel Tower in Paris, it was an instant success, and crowds flocked to see this engineering masterpiece. It is hardly surprising, therefore, that in 1920 the Dunlop Guide describes Blackpool as 'the most popular seaside resort in England: scene of the holiday revels of Manchester, Liverpool, and the industrial centres of Lancashire generally. Blackpool has gone into the 'business' of catering for the millions ...'

In the photograph on the left (53853) we see that the North Pier now has its new large pavilion straddling the entrance. We can also see something of the new sea wall, built as the Promenade was progressively widened from the early 1900s onwards. Much of the work was carried out to the plan of the then Borough Engineer, James Brodie.

The world-famous Tower (right, 43333) was inspired by Gustave Eiffel's great tower in Paris, which had opened five years earlier; but at 518 feet, Blackpool Tower is only a little over half its height. However, it boasted a ballroom, a permanent circus and an aquarium incorporated within the building at its base.

Left: BLACKPOOL, FROM THE NORTH PIER 1906 53853

Right: BLACKPOOL, THE TOWER FROM CENTRAL PIER 1899 43333p

AS JUSTICE Shallow might say, Blackpool has two piers, and everything handsome about it. Both are large; the north one is the more select, and the south more popular – just a penny pier where dancing goes on all day in the summer. The promenade is lighted by electricity, and has an electric tramway. Not to be left behind in any respect, Blackpool now has an Eiffel Tower of its own. A rate was raised for giving the town's attractions wide advertisement through the medium of handbills and flaring posters; one would hardly think, however, that this was the best way of drawing the most satisfactory class of visitors to 'the finest promenade in England'. Standing solidly upon a low range of cliffs, facing the Irish Sea, Blackpool enjoys its briny breezes for nine months of the year. At low tide the grasping waves retire nearly half a mile, leaving a stretch of sand nearly twenty miles in length. The amusements on this extensive beach include riding and driving.

VICTORIAN GUIDEBOOK

Opposite above:
BLACKPOOL, THE FLYING MACHINE 1906 *53857*

Opposite below:
BLACKPOOL, THE WINTER GARDENS 1890 *22892*

Above:
BLACKPOOL, THE SOUTH JETTY FROM THE WELLINGTON
HOTEL 1890 *22881*

ABOVE (22881) we see the South Jetty, taken from a room in the Wellington Hotel. Opened in 1868, the jetty was a regular call for excursion steamers from Liverpool, Llandudno and Morecambe Bay. When the Victoria Pier was opened in 1893, the jetty was renamed the Central Pier.

The Pleasure Beach actually started as a fairground on the South Shore. One of the early rides was the Sir Hiram Maxim Flying Machine (opposite left, 53857). The ride was built in 1904, and hurtled round at an exhilarating 40mph.

The Winter Gardens (left, 22892) opened in 1878 as part of the town's attempt at culture. Facilities included a library, an art gallery and a reading room, which together with plays, concerts and lectures combined to offer the genteel some sort of safe haven from the masses.

WORDSWORTH'S LAKES

Cumbria

THE poet William Wordsworth lived with his sister Dorothy at Dove Cottage, just outside Grasmere, from 1799 to 1813. He wrote some of his best-known poetry here. The cottage is now part of a museum dedicated to the life and work of the poet – the founder of the Lakeland Romantic Movement. Thomas de Quincey was a lifelong friend of the poet, and his painstaking account of the cottage he was later to live in himself is given here.

Wordsworth was a true solitary – the early photograph (left, 18663) conjures up the extraordinary atmosphere of the Lakes he relished. He composed his poetry whilst walking the fells, and loved the silence and remoteness of his beloved Lakes. He was forever worried that they would be overrun by visitors, and by incomers building villas on the exposed flanks of hills overlooking the lakes. He was particularly concerned when the railway was about to arrive. He wrote to the builders of the Kendal and Windermere Railway: 'Is there no nook of English ground secure from rash assault?' The culprits were in many cases the mill owners, sending their workers on day trips to break the monotony of the factory slog. Wordsworth wrote that the appreciation of the Lakes is a 'cultivated taste … surely that good is not to be obtained by transferring at once uneducated persons in large bodies to particular spots?'

It seems nothing is new. Once can sympathise with the poet, but also with the plain working people of Lancashire, keen to broaden their own horizons and gain a little joy out of their hard lives.

KESWICK AND DERWENT WATER

WORDSWORTH'S DOVE COTTAGE

It was, in its exterior, not so much a picturesque cottage – for its outline and proportions, its windows and its chimneys, were not sufficiently marked and effective for the picturesque – as it was lovely: one gable end was, indeed, most gorgeously apparelled in ivy, and so far picturesque; but the principal side, or what might be called front, as it presented itself to the road, and was most illuminated by windows, was embossed – nay, it might be said, smothered – in roses of different species, amongst which the moss and the damask prevailed. These, together with as much jessamine and honeysuckle as could find room to flourish, were not only in themselves a most interesting garniture for a humble cottage wall, but they also performed the acceptable service of breaking the unpleasant glare that would else have wounded the eye from the whitewash; a glare which, having been renewed amongst the general preparations against my coming to inhabit the house, could not be sufficiently subdued in tone for the artist's eye until the storm of several winters had weather-stained and tamed down its brilliancy.

THOMAS DE QUINCEY (1785–1859)

Opposite left:
WINDERMERE 1886 *18663p*

Above:
GRASMERE, DOVE COTTAGE
1936 *87636*

Right:
HAWKSHEAD, THE GRAMMAR
SCHOOL 1892 *30538*
Here Wordsworth went to school.

WILLIAM WORDSWORTH
'THE PRELUDE BOOK 1' 1799

WISDOM and Spirit of the universe!
Thou Soul that art the eternity of thought
That givest to forms and images a breath
And everlasting motion, not in vain
By day or star-light thus from my first dawn
Of childhood didst thou intertwine for me
The passions that build up our human soul;
Not with the mean and vulgar works of man,
But with high objects, with enduring things –
With life and nature – purifying thus
The elements of feeling and of thought,

And sanctifying, by such discipline,
Both pain and fear, until we recognise
A grandeur in the beatings of the heart.
Nor was this fellowship vouchsafed to me
With stinted kindness. In November days,
When vapours rolling down the valley made
A lonely scene more lonesome, among woods,
At noon and 'mid the calm of summer nights,
When, by the margin of the trembling lake,
Beneath the gloomy hills homeward I went
In solitude, such intercourse was mine;
Mine was it in the fields both day and night,
And by the waters, all the summer long.

THE steam ferry leaves Ferry Nab with two horse-drawn vehicles on board (right, 38802), with the chain used in propulsion clearly visible. Owing to occasional mishaps with this chain, it was later replaced by the present-day double hawser system. The shed-like superstructure of the boat houses the steam boiler. Quite unperturbed by the noise and wash created by the ferry, a long-skirted woman fishes with rod and line from a little promontory.

The tiny hump-backed bridge at Ashness (below right, 32871) on the narrow road which leads up from the eastern shore of Derwent Water to the Norse hamlet of Watendlath has been seen on countless Lake District calendars, but this must be one of the earliest photographs. The bold profile of Skiddaw fills the background across the lake.

View 20470 (below) looks across White Cross Bay to the northern end of the lake. On the shore to the right a factory for the construction of Sunderland flying boats was established during the Second World War. The number on the rowing boat is evidence of the 19th-century regulation of boating on the lake. The 1881 census recorded Thomas Walker, whose name is painted on the boat, as a boat builder.

Opposite:
WASTWATER, ON THE SHORE 1889 *22110p*

Above:
BOWNESS-ON-WINDERMERE, THE FERRY BOAT 1896 *38802*

Left:
WINDERMERE, FROM CALGARTH 1887 *20470*

Right:
DERWENT WATER, ASHNESS BRIDGE 1893 *32871*

ONCE a vital part of Durham's defences, the river in more recent times has been used for more pleasurable purposes. Boating is a popular pastime, and the river is used by a variety of pleasure and competitive craft. In the foreground we see a couple of moored rowing boats that would be used to take lady friends for a gentle meander along the river on a fine, sunny afternoon, whereas on the river are a couple of skiffs that would be used for more competitive purposes. The picturesque building below the cathedral is the old fulling mill, standing beside its weir. Once the property of the priors of Durham, the fulling mill was once known as the Jesus Mill; it now houses the Durham University Museum of Archaeology. The mill dates from the start of the 15th century, when it played its part in the growing weaving trade at that time. During the 1950s it was a popular riverside café. Then it was converted into the present-day museum, where exhibits illustrate the early history of Durham and the surrounding area.

DURHAM

County Durham

THE historic significance of Durham is inexorably linked with its being regarded as the cradle of Christianity in England. It was the resting place of the precious body of St Cuthbert, who died in 687.

When William the Conqueror finally took control of Durham, he combined the powers of the bishop and the Earl of Northumbria to create Durham's first prince bishop, a Norman called William Walcher. Walcher's leadership was weak, which ultimately resulted in his being murdered at Gateshead in 1081. His replacement was William St Carileph, the man responsible for building the present cathedral, which occupies the site of the old stone minster built by Uchted. Carileph began its construction in 1093. He designed the greater part of the cathedral as it stands today; the new building was completed to the bishop's designs in around 40 years.

The Norman interior of the cathedral is lavish and imposing. At the far end of the choir (left, 30745) is the high altar. Above it is the magnificent rose window, over 98ft in circumference. It shows Christ, 'the Saviour of the World', as the inscription says, surrounded by the 12 apostles and the 24 elders from the Book of Revelation.

Old Elvet (below left, 67127) was once the site of the city's horse fair. The street is unusually wide and spacious for Durham; it was further extended in the 1960s, when road development saw the demise of the Waterloo Hotel, the building beyond the Royal County Hotel (right). The fountain of 1863 in the centre of the photograph disappeared before the Second World War.

Opposite:
DURHAM, THE CATHEDRAL FROM THE
RIVER 1921 *70712t*

Above left:
DURHAM CATHEDRAL, THE CHOIR,
LOOKING EAST 1892 *30745*

Left:
DURHAM, OLD ELVET 1914 *67127*

Right:
DURHAM CATHEDRAL, THE NORTH DOOR,
THE SANCTUARY KNOCKER C1877 *9434*

STEPHENSON'S RAILWAY

Darlington, Co Durham

DESIGNED and built by George Stephenson, Stockton & Darlington No 1, 'Locomotion', achieved a maximum speed of 15mph when she hauled the 34-wagon inaugural train from Shildon to Stockton on 27 September 1825. 'Locomotion' was one of the stars of the S & D Railway centenary celebrations in 1925, though the old girl was not quite herself; her power came from a hidden petrol engine, and the smoke from her chimney was burning oily waste.

'Derwent' was designed and built by Alfred Kitchen at his foundry near North Road Station. She entered service with the S & D Railway in 1843, two years after 'Locomotion' had been retired. Both locomotives are now housed in the Darlington Railway Centre & Museum, North Road Station.

Opposite: DARLINGTON, 'THE LOCOMOTION' 1892 *30646*

Above: DARLINGTON, 'THE DERWENT' 1901 *48014*

We clung on by the front springs of the carriage, screaming 'fire' incessantly ...

ON THE 8th of December I left Darlington by the 9h 25m train for London. I travelled in my chariot with my maid. The carriage was strapped on to a truck and placed with its back to the engine, about the centre of the train, which was a long one. Soon after leaving Leicester I thought I smelt something burning and told my maid to look out of the window on her side to see if anything was on fire. She let down the window, and so many lumps of red-hot coal or coke were showering down that she put it up again immediately. I still thought I smelt something burning; she put down the window again and exclaimed that the carriage was on fire. We then put down the side-windows and waved our handkerchiefs, screaming 'fire' as loud as we could. No one took any notice of us. I then pulled up the windows, lest the current of air through the carriage should cause the fire to burn more rapidly into the carriage, and determined to sit in as long as possible. After some time, seeing that no assistance was likely to be afforded us, my maid became terrified, and without telling me her intention, opened the door, let down the step, and scrambled out on to the truck. We clung on by the front springs of the carriage, screaming 'fire' incessantly, and waving our handkerchiefs. We passed several policemen on the road, none of whom took any notice of us. No guard appeared.

THE COUNTESS OF ZETLAND 1847

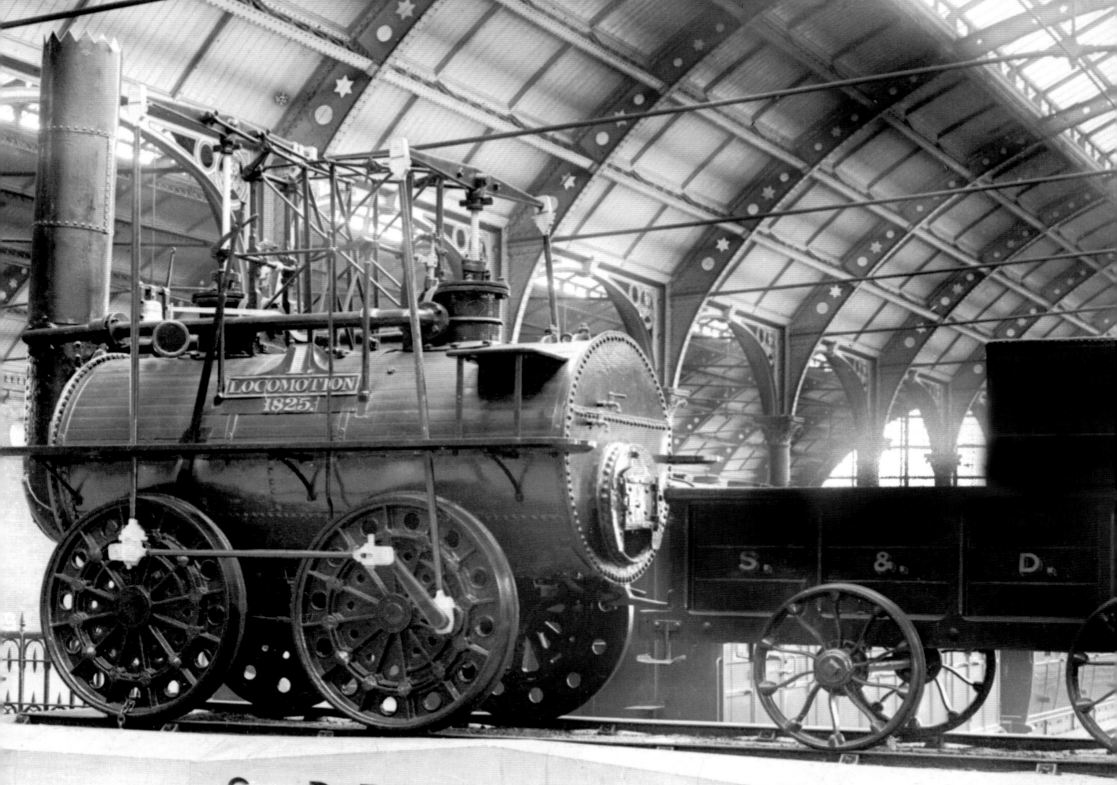

LOCOMOTION
1825.

S. & D.

S. & D. R. Nº I. 1825.

NEWCASTLE-UPON-TYNE
Tyne & Wear

AT THE beginning of the 20th century, British shipyards were at the forefront of world shipbuilding. In its heyday, the region around Newcastle and the Tyne was a hive of heavy industry. There were dozens of coal mines working, shipyards still lined the banks of the Tyne and the Wear, railway locomotives were being built at Heaton, and armoured vehicles at Elswick.

In the photograph of the quayside (below left, N16320) the late 19th-century skyline of Newcastle is dominated by the 15th-century tower and spire of St Nicholas's Cathedral and the imposing bulk of the castle keep.

The arrival of a ship for loading or unloading brought the quayside to life (opposite left, N16316). The steam lorry belonging to brewers William McEwan & Co might be a clue to the cargo. McEwans was founded in 1856 at the Fountain brewery, Edinburgh. The beers were sold under two names, McEwans and Younger.

When the late 18th-century bridge over the Tyne was demolished in the 1870s to make way for the swing bridge (left, N16318), traces of an earlier medieval bridge and a Roman bridge were discovered. The swing bridge cost £288,000 to build and has an overall length of 560ft. The swing section is 281ft, giving two navigable channels each 104ft wide. The superstructure was designed and built by Sir W G Armstrong at Elswick and was floated into place.

Opposite left:
NEWCASTLE,
THE QUAYSIDE 1928
N16316

Above:
NEWCASTLE,
THE SWING BRIDGE 1890
N16318

Left:
NEWCASTLE,
THE QUAYSIDE 1896
N16320

Right:
NEWCASTLE, THE CASTLE
1901 *N16322*

THE ROMAN WALL
Northumberland

Verily I have seene the tract of it over the high pitches and steepe descents of hilles, wonderfully rising and falling. I have observ'd the track of it running up the mountains and down again, in a most surprising manner.

WILLIAM CAMDEN, 'BRITANNIA', 1586

Above: GILSLAND, THE ROMAN WALL, CRAG LOUGH 1924 76662p

Right: BARDON MILL, A ROMAN MILE STONE 1924 76665

Opposite top: GILSLAND, THE VICARAGE, ROMAN ALTARS AND STONES 1924 76660

Opposite below: CHOLLERFORD, RECESSES IN ROMAN CAMP, CILURNUM, CHESTERS 1924 76659

HADRIAN'S Wall was painstakingly built out of stone and turf by the Romans around AD 120. It was created to span the entire width of Great Britain and so prevent military invasions from the north by the Pictish tribes of Scotland. It also succeeded in stabilising the regional economy and encouraging peace among the various factions. It clearly defined the physical frontier that separated the savage Selgovae tribe in the north from the Brigantes in the south. This was a clever move by the Romans, for it discouraged the tribes from forming a united force.

The wall was the northern border of the Roman Empire in Britain for hundreds of years, and was certainly the most heavily defended fortification in the Empire. Trade and commerce, of course, had to go on, and there were gates through the wall with customs posts so that merchandise could be authorised and taxed accordingly.

This impressive stretch of Hadrian's Wall is near Gilsland (opposite, 76662). Crag Lough is situated beneath the cliffs of Whin Sill, which gives dramatic views to the walkers following the wall. For rock climbing enthusiasts, this area is the best in Northumberland.

Bardon Mill (below, 76665) is the highest point of Hadrian's Wall at 345 metres. The Roman fort of Vindolanda stands between here and Once Brewed. The lookout and signalling post on the crest of Windshields commanded a vast uninterrupted view, but it would have been extremely windy.

ROMAN HELMETS

ROBERT BURNS

Dumfries & Galloway

SCOTLAND'S most celebrated poet Robert Burns was born in this simple cottage (right) on 25 January 1759. The cottage, a 'but and ben' or two-room clay cottage, was built by the poet's father, a gardener from Kincardineshire. It later became an inn. Burns's verses are famous the world over. He died at the early age of 37 in Dumfries. In 1881 the cottage was purchased by the trustees of the Burns Monument and opened as a museum. The pleasant village of Alloway is now the centre of pilgrimage for lovers of Burns's poetry.

WHEN chapman billies leave the street,
And drouthy neibors, neibors, meet;
As market days are wearing late,
And folk begin to tak the gate,
While we sit bousing at the nappy,
An' getting fou and unco happy,
We think na on the lang Scots miles,
The mosses, waters, slaps and stiles,
That lie between us and our hame,
Where sits our sulky, sullen dame,
Gathering her brows like gathering storm,
Nursing her wrath to keep it warm.
This truth fand honest Tam o' Shanter,
As he frae Ayr ae night did canter:
(Auld Ayr, wham ne'er a town surpasses,
For honest men and bonie lasses).
O Tam! had'st thou but been sae wise,
As taen thy ain wife Kate's advice!
She tauld thee weel thou was a skellum,
A blethering, blustering, drunken blellum …
That at the Lord's house, ev'n on Sunday,
Thou drank wi' Kirkton Jean till Monday,
She prophesied that late or soon,
Thou wad be found, deep drown'd in Doon,
Or catch'd wi' warlocks in the mirk,
By Alloway's auld, haunted kirk.

ROBERT BURNS, FROM 'TAM O'SHANTER'

Above:
ALLOWAY,
THE BIRTHPLACE OF
ROBERT BURNS 1897
39858

Right:
ALLOWAY,
THE BURNS MONUMENT
1897 *39863*

Opposite:
ALLOWAY,
THE KIRK 1897 *39861*

Robert Burns played in this churchyard as a boy, and the popular legends about hauntings and the ghostly atmosphere of the roofless ruin affected him deeply. He used the kirk and the Auld Brig o'Doon near by as scenes for his celebrated ghost story 'Tam O' Shanter', which first appeared in The Edinburgh Review in 1791 (excerpt on opposite page). Burns's father, who had repaired the kirk wall to keep the sheep at bay, is buried in the churchyard.

HERE, within the heartland of Glasgow's commercial and financial life, the imposing Victorian buildings we see are still standing today. We are looking towards George Square, and in the hazy background of the photograph one of the domes of the City Chambers is just visible. Nearby are the National Bank, the Royal Exchange, the Stock Exchange, and the Athenaeum Club. It was the advent of steam power that saw the development of Glasgow's two greatest industries – shipbuilding and railway locomotives. The shipyards included John Brown & Co of Clydebank, A & J Inglis Ltd and D & W Henderson & Co. Railway locomotives were manufactured by the North British Locomotive Co, an amalgamation of three companies employing 7,000 workers. In total, the NBL built about 20,000 railway locomotives for customers world-wide.

At the Broomielaw (opposite above, 39799) Glaswegian workers and their families embarked on welcome day trips and holidays to Rothesay and Dunoon. The Glasgow & Inverary and the Loch Goil & Loch Long Steamboat Companies sported the same colour scheme: black hull and paddle boxes with white saloons and lifeboats. The funnel colour was red, with two white bands enclosing a black one. The top of the funnel was also painted black.

GLASGOW
Strathclyde

DESPITE its cathedral founded in 1136, and the university founded in 1451, by the mid 15th century Glasgow was little known outside Scotland, and then only as a place of learning and Christian culture.

The advent of overseas trade, particularly with the American colonies, resulted in textile and tobacco businesses flourishing in the 18th century. The geographical advantage of Glasgow's position straddling the river Clyde meant that the Industrial Revolution in the following century witnessed huge expansion of heavy engineering, steel and ironworks, shipbuilding, and locomotive steam engines.

Looking along the Broomielaw (below right, 39801) towards Clyde Street, this picture gives us a good view of the railway bridge serving Central Station, whilst immediately behind it work is under way on rebuilding Glasgow Bridge. It is also possible to make out the towers of the suspension bridge situated a little further along the river. On the far bank are some of the warehouses along Bridge Wharf.

In the centre of George Square (below left, 39759) the column of Sir Walter Scott dominates. The large building in the centre background is the Merchants' House, opened in 1877. Upper storeys have since been added. There are many statues of famous Victorian figures, including the only equestrian statue of Queen Victoria ever made. Prince Albert (also on horseback) is nearby.

THE bustle of trade, the closely ranked houses, the smoke and the stir, together make a change from the open river banks which is more striking than agreeable. The Clyde has lost its mountain purity.
VICTORIAN GUIDEBOOK

Opposite:
GLASGOW, ST VINCENT PLACE, LOOKING EAST 1897 *39764t*

Above:
GLASGOW, AT THE BROOMIELAW 1897 *39799*

Right:
GLASGOW, LOOKING ALONG THE BROOMIELAW TOWARDS CLYDE STREET 1897 *39801*

Left:
GLASGOW, GEORGE SQUARE 1897 *39759*

ROTHESAY

Argyll and Bute

ROTHESAY is in an ideal location in the sheltered 'sweet Rothesay Bay', to quote the popular song. It is the county town on the eastern side of the Island of Bute. The pier has changed little from how it appears in this photograph: in the holiday period it is still as busy as it was a century ago. The main sailing destinations from Rothesay are to Wemyss Bay on the Ayrshire coast and, in the summer season, to the Island of Arran.

In the summer months the resort was always busy with steamers arriving from Glasgow's Broomielaw.

The tram and tramlines in photograph 39837 (below right) are gone now, but the buildings and the main hotels still exist. The Victorian elegance has given way to more casual fashions, and horse-drawn vehicles have all but disappeared. The pier continues to cater for steamer excursions, and there are ample opportunities for the sea angler. The town also boasts winter gardens, a swimming pool, dancing, and golf.

A week's stay at the Glenburn Hydropathic (below right, 43210) cost around 59s. Although guests were not obliged to take any of the water treatments offered, they were expected to refrain from drinking alcohol, and had to take their meals together at prescribed hours.

Above:
ROTHESAY,
THE ESPLANADE 1897
39837

Right:
ROTHESAY,
THE GLENBURN
HYDROPATHIC 1899
43210

Opposite:
ROTHESAY, THE PIER
1897 *39836*

The Day We Went to Rothesay

THE Day We Went to Rothesay,
O One Hogmany at Glesca Fair
There was me, mysel' and sev'ral mair
We a' went off to hae a tear
And spend the nicht in Rothesay, O.
We wander'd through the Broomilaw
Thro' wind and rain and sleet and snaw

And at forty minutes after twa
We got the length of Rothesay, O

A dirrum a doo a dum a day
A dirrum a doo a daddy, O
A dirrum a doo a dum a day
The day we spent in Rothesay, O.

TRADITIONAL

On the calm sea, on a fine summer evening, the whole water is covered with boats and vessels; the dark sails of the former, no less than their beautiful pyramidal outline, sprinkling the whole blue expanse in every variety of combination ... VICTORIAN GUIDEBOOK

ISLE OF ARRAN
North Ayrshire

THE island of Arran is about 20 miles in length by 12 in breadth, and a large district occupying much of the northern half still remains as mountain moorland … On the calm sea, on a fine summer evening, the whole water is covered with boats and vessels; the dark sails of the former, no less than their beautiful pyramidal outline, sprinkling the whole blue expanse in every variety of combination and of magnitude. Within the bay, the different groups are disposed nearer the eye in a thousand picturesque assemblages, varying at every moment, as they are hoisting their sails to stand out to sea, or as they run alongside the sloops where the flag is flying to receive their cargoes. On shore crowds of men, women and children surround the sail-tents, where the smoke of the fires scattered along the margin of the water is ascending to the hills, mixing with the evening mists, and contrasting with the yellow of the setting sun.

VICTORIAN GUIDEBOOK

LOCH Ranza (opposite, A93001) is a sea-loch that forms an inlet of the Kilbrannan Sound. This view was photographed near the northern tip of the island. Lochranza Castle dates from the late 13th century to the mid 14th century with 16th-century additions, and features one of the earliest examples of an added jamb or wing which was built on to increase the castle's defence capability. The square tower projects to cover the entrance, and is equipped with long arrow slits of an early design. The original entrance was of the heavily ribbed barrel-vaulted type. It was here that Robert Bruce is said to have landed on his return from Ireland in 1306.

Now owned by the National Trust for Scotland, Brodick Castle (below, A93002), once the seat of the Dukes of Hamilton, dates from the 14th century. It was from here in 1307 that the Bruce launched his campaign to liberate mainland Scotland from the English. Brodick was enlarged when garrisoned by Cromwell's troops, and the tower is a mid 19th-century addition.

179

THE FORTH BRIDGE

Lothian

QUEENSFERRY is so called because this passage across the Firth was frequently used by Margaret, queen of Malcolm Canmore. From the Fifeshire shore a promontory juts out, diminishing the breadth of the channel by about one half, so that from shore to shore is less than two miles. In former days this was one of the most beautiful parts of the Firth. The little islands dotted on the water, the woods of Donibristle, the houses of Inverkeithing, and the ruined castle of Rosyth standing at the water's edge, afforded many pleasant prospects. The great railway viaduct across the Firth, from North to South Queensferry, is a splendid triumph of engineering, for the intervals between its piers are unusually great, and it is lofty enough to allow ships of considerable size to pass beneath. Now that this is completed and the Tay Bridge rebuilt, the county is both entered and left by a viaduct of exceptional magnitude.

VICTORIAN GUIDEBOOK

DESIGNED by Sir John Fowler and Sir Benjamin Baker, the Forth Bridge cost £3,000,000 to build. Of the workforce of 4,500 men, 57 were killed in work-related accidents. Construction of the bridge began in November 1882. The first test trains ran from January 1890, and the official opening took place on 4 March 1890. The bridge is more than 2,760 yards long, including the approach viaducts, giving a clear headway at high water of 150 ft. The steel towers stand 360 ft high and are supported on granite piers. The deepest foundations are 88 ft below high water.

Left:
THE FORTH BRIDGE 1897 39142

Opposite:
THE FORTH BRIDGE 1897 39145

EDINBURGH
Lothian

EDINBURGH became Scotland's capital without ceremony more than 500 years ago when James II decided to hold his parliament in the town. Edinburgh (Old Town) was quite small, consisting of only a few hundred houses huddled in close proximity to the eastern side of the castle. Just when Edinburgh was founded is open to speculation. The name is thought to be derived from 'Edwin's burgh'; Edwin was an early 7th-century king of Northumbria. At that time, Northumbria was all-powerful. Its territory extended from the Forth to the Humber, and Edwin is known to have fortified a part of the area occupied by the present castle. He also encouraged a civilian settlement nearby. Under David I, Edinburgh was a royal burgh, which brought with it a number of trading privileges. In David's day, church and state were interlinked; it was David who re-introduced monasticism back into Scotland.

A BATTALION of the Black Watch parades on the castle esplanade (above, 39121a). Raised by General Wade in 1725, the Black Watch was formally constituted as a regiment of the line in 1739, and its strength was increased from four to ten companies.

The Edinburgh Castle we see today is, with a few additions, that built by the Earl of Morton following the siege of 1572 (right, E24506). Morton succeeded Lennox as Regent, and took the fortress in the name of the infant James VI from the supporters of Mary, Queen of Scots. It was Morton who added the great half-moon battery to the castle's defences.

The Grassmarket (left, 39121) was the site of many an execution and the location of the Porteous Riots in 1736. John Porteous was appointed captain of one of the companies employed to keep the peace. At a riot following the execution of a man named Robertson, Porteous ordered his men to fire on the crowd. He was later taken into custody, tried and condemned to death.

Opposite:
EDINBURGH, THE CASTLE FROM THE GRASSMARKET 1897 *39121t*

Above:
EDINBURGH, THE BLACKWATCH ON THE CASTLE ESPLANADE 1897 *39121a*

Right:
EDINBURGH, THE CASTLE AND THE NATIONAL GALLERY 1897 *E24506*

CONSIDERED to be one of the finest boulevards in Europe, Princes Street (above, 39113) was the place to shop and eat. Restaurants included a branch of Ferguson & Forrester, the Royal British, and Littlejohn's. Confectioners included Mackies, and also Ritchies, where shortbread was a speciality. At the turn of the 20th century Princes Street boasted a number of hotels. The most expensive to stay at was the North British at Waverley Station. Next on the list were the Caledonian, the Station and the Royal, followed by the somewhat cheaper Royal British, the Douglas and the Bedford. There was also the Old Waverley, which was a temperance establishment.

The building of Holyroodhouse (opposite, 39168) was started in about 1500 by James IV; the work continued under James V, who added a new tower and quadrangle. In May 1544, the palace was badly damaged when it was set on fire by the Earl of Hertford's troops. Extensive alterations to the palace were undertaken between 1670 and 1679 by Sir William Bruce, the king's surveyor in Scotland. The strong French influence in Sir William's designs reflected Charles II's passion for things Gallic. The dominating mass of Arthur's Seat, 822 ft high, stands in a 648-acre park.

I looked down on the whole city and firth – the sun then setting behind the magnificent rock, crested by the castle.

I CLIMBED last night to the crags just below Arthur's Seat — itself a rude triangle-shaped-base cliff, and looked down on the whole city and firth — the sun then setting behind the magnificent rock, crested by the castle. The firth was full of ships, and I counted fifty-four heads of mountains, of which at least forty-four were cones or pyramids. The smoke was rising from ten thousand houses, each smoke from some one family. It was an affecting sight to me! I stood gazing at the setting sun, so tranquil to a passing look, and so restless and vibrating to one who looked steadfast; and then, all at once, turning my eyes down upon the city, it and all its smokes and figures became all at once dipped in the brightest blue-purple: such a sight that I almost grieved when my eyes recovered their natural tone! Meantime, Arthur's Crag, close behind me, was in dark blood-like crimson, and the sharpshooters were behind exercising minutely, and had chosen that place on account of the fine thunder echo which, indeed, it would be scarcely possible for the ear to distinguish from thunder. The passing a day or two, quite unknown, in a strange city, does a man's heart good. He rises 'a sadder and a wiser man'.

SAMUEL TAYLOR COLERIDGE
LETTER TO ROBERT SOUTHEY 13 SEPTEMBER 1803

Opposite:
EDINBURGH, PRINCES STREET 1897   *39113t*

Above:
EDINBURGH, HOLYROOD PALACE AND ARTHUR'S SEAT 1897   *39168*

Right:
EDINBURGH, HOLYROOD PALACE, KING CHARLES'S BEDROOM 1897   *39172*

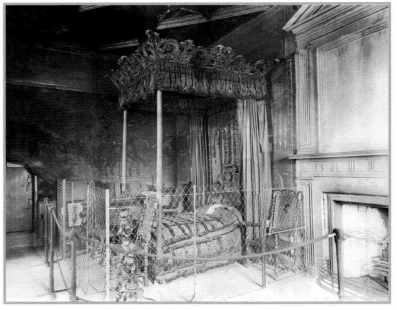

IONA
Highlands

IONA lies just off the extreme south-west of Mull. In 1203, the Benedictines founded a monastery on the island which lasted until the Reformation. In 1899, the 8th Duke of Argyll presented the ruins of the abbey to the Church of Scotland in the hope that restoration work might be undertaken. The building was eventually re-roofed, and used for worship again in 1910.

It was chosen by St Columba in AD 563 as the site for a religious house from where he could carry out his missionary work. St Columba was a member of the O'Neill clan; he left Ireland after the battle of Cuil-dremne. It is said that it was Columba himself who caused the battle: he was accused by the High King of taking a psalter without permission, so Columba appealed to his clan for help in clearing his name, and the matter was settled by sword and axe.

The ruined Romanesque chapel stands by the graveyard. Iona is the oldest Christian burial ground in Scotland, and contains the graves of many kings and chieftains.

At Iona, the storm howls among its crumbling walls; its massive tower stands four square to all the winds that blow.

VICTORIAN GUIDEBOOK

Above:
IONA,
THE CATHEDRAL
1903 *50889*

Below left:
IONA, COTTAGES BY
THE SHORE 1903
50887

Opposite:
IONA, ST ORAN'S
CHAPEL 1903 *50892*

THE ruins are very different from those of most of the abbeys of England: instead of nestling in some sheltered dale, they stand on the wind-smitten shore of the bare and rocky isle; no groves of trees cluster around their grey walls, half-hiding them from the passer-by, nor does mantling ivy mask the rents which time and man have made. At Iona, the storm howls among its crumbling walls; its massive tower stands four square to all the winds that blow.

VICTORIAN GUIDEBOOK

A hut is constructed with loose stones, ranged for the most part with some tendency to circularity. It must be placed where the wind cannot act upon it with violence, because it has no cement; and where the water will run easily away, because it has no floor but the naked ground. The wall, which is commonly about six feet high, declines from the perpendicular a little inward. Such rafters as can be procured are then raised for a roof, and covered with heath, which makes a strong and warm thatch, kept from flying off by ropes of twisted heath, of which the ends, reaching from the centre of the thatch to the top of the wall, are held firm by the weight of a large stone. No light is admitted but at the entrance, and through a hole in the thatch, which gives vent to the smoke … Such is the general structure of the houses in which one of the nations of this opulent and powerful island has been hitherto content to live.

SAMUEL JOHNSON, 'A JOURNEY TO THE WESTERN ISLES OF SCOTLAND', 1775

IN THE HIGHLANDS

THE scenery of the Scottish Highlands is unequalled. Throughout are ancient castles, broad placid lochs, rugged mountains and picturesque isolated villages.

The 13th-century castle at Inverlochy (left, I30001), home of the Comyn family, is built in the form of a square, with round towers at the corners. Set on the banks of the River Lochy, it is one of Scotland's earliest stone castles, and it was here in February 1645, after a forced march across difficult terrain in appalling weather, that the Marquis of Montrose with 1,500 troops defeated a 5,000-strong force of Campbells and Lowlanders. The clan power of Argyll is said to have been destroyed for a generation.

At Kyleakin on the Isle of Skye (below left, K53001) stand the ruins of Castle Moil. It is said that the castle was built by the daughter of one of the Norse kings of the Western Isles. Legend has it that she had a boom placed across the strait, and any ship plying between Skye and the mainland had to pay a toll. The town overlooks the narrow strait of Kyle Akin, which is said to take its name from King Haakon who sailed this way in 1263.

The hugely impressive mountain of Ben Cruachan (below, I15303), its summit 1126m above sea level, boasts two Munros (peaks over 3,000 feet in height), and it is one of the most celebrated mountains in Scotland, with its dramatic ridges and steep, soaring cliffs. The climb to the great dam of Cruachan Reservoir is popular with walkers, who ascend the steep paths through beautiful woodland, passing these tumbling falls.

Opposite:
GLENCOE, COTTAGES
1890 *43199*

Above:
INVERLOCHY, THE CASTLE
C1890 *I30001*

Left:
ISLE OF SKYE, KYLEAKIN
C1890 *K53001*

Right:
INVERARY, THE FALLS OF
CRUACHAN C1955 *I15303*

THE town of Strathpeffer owes its popularity to the discovery of sulphurous springs in the 18th century. These were declared by medical practitioners in the Victorian era to be the most curative in Britain. The village rapidly grew into a popular spa town, with visitors flocking from all over Europe to sample its sulphur and chalybeate springs. It was served by a branch line of the Highland Railway from Fodderty Junction. Are these girls laundresses at one of the hotels?

YESTERDAY it was perfectly horrific. It had rained all night ... Through the whole glen, which is ten miles long, torrents were boiling and foaming, and sending up in every direction spray like the smoke of great fires. They were rushing down every hill and mountainside, and tearing like devils across the path.

CHARLES KINGSLEY, 1862

ON a stormy day, Glencoe can seem the wildest, most bleak spot on earth. One Victorian account describes it vividly: 'Trees and cultivated fields are left behind, rolling masses of ice-worn rock form the floor of the glen, which slopes quickly upwards towards the base of great cliffs and rugged mountain masses ... The name is said to mean the Pass of Weeping – a term too truly prophetic, for, as is well known, the Massacre of Glencoe is a dark stain upon the annals of our country'.

Glencoe village stands on the shores of Loch Leven. The reason for the massacre was the failure of MacIan to swear allegiance to William III before 1 January 1692. MacIan had arrived at Fort William on 31 December, but was redirected to Inverary, with the result that he did not take the oath until 6 January. The result was that at dawn on 13 February 1692, soldiers commanded by Campbell of Glen Lyon killed at least 40 out of the 200 MacDonalds living in this glen. Among the dead was the MacDonald chieftain MacIan of Glencoe himself, who was buried on the island of Eilean Munde.

A FEW miles to the south of Nairn stands Cawdor Castle (right, C212001), one of Scotland's finest medieval buildings. It is famous for its association with Macbeth and the murder of Duncan. The central tower of the castle dates from a licence of 1454 when the thane was permitted to erect Cawdor 'with walls and ditches and equip the summit with turrets and means of defence, with warlike provisions and strengths ... provided that it would always be open and ready for the King's use and his successors'. Cawdor is traditionally the scene of Duncan's murder by Macbeth, Thane of Cawdor. The castle was extensively altered during the 16th and 17th centuries and again in the 19th.

Opposite:
STRATHPEFFER, WASHING DAY c1890 *S421003p*

Above:
GLENCOE 1890 *G81001*

Left:
CAWDOR CASTLE 1890 *C212001*

LYING to the north-east of Iona, the uninhabited island of Staffa is famous for its caves and rock formations. Legend has it that the cave was formed when the giant Finn Mcoul made the island. Finn is also said to have built the Giant's Causeway in Northern Ireland. Sir Walter Scott visited the phenomenon and said that it was 'one of the most extraordinary places I ever beheld. It exceeded, in my mind, every description I had heard of it ... composed entirely of basaltic pillars as high as the roof of a cathedral, and running deep into the rock, eternally swept by a deep and swelling sea, and paved, as it were, with ruddy marble, it baffles all description'.

WE were put out into boats and lifted by the hissing sea up the pillar stumps to the celebrated Fingal's Cave. A greener roar of waves surely never rushed into a stranger cavern – its many pillars making it look like the inside of an immense organ, black and resounding, and absolutely without purpose, and quite alone, the wide grey sea within and without.

FELIX MENDELSSOHN 1829

A greener roar of waves surely never rushed into a stranger cavern – its many pillars making it look like the inside of an immense organ ...

THE road south from Braemar (left, B266003) climbs through Glen Clunie and then over the rugged Cairnwell Pass, the highest point on a main road in Britain, and now the main A93 between Aberdeenshire and Perthshire. Here there are scenes of breathtaking beauty, and herds of wild red deer roam among the mountains.

Braemar Castle (right, B266001) is a five-storey L-plan tower-house built by the Earl of Mar in 1628. It was here in August 1714 that a so-called hunt was assembled by John Erskine, sixth Earl of Mar. It was in fact the start of a rebellion against the house of Hanover and the Union, and the Stuart standard was raised. Though Braemar had been burnt by Graham of Claverhouse in 1689, it had been rebuilt. The curtain wall was added when the castle was used as a garrison for government troops.

AT a quarter past seven o'clock we arrived at dear Balmoral. Strange, very strange, it seemed to me to drive past—indeed, through the old house, the connecting part between it and the offices being broken through. The new house looks beautiful; the tower and the rooms in the connecting part are, however, only half furnished, and the offices are still unbuilt, therefore the gentlemen (except the minister) live in the old house. There is a long wooden passage which connects the new house with the offices. An old shoe was thrown after us into the house, for good luck, when we entered the hall. The house is charming, the rooms delightful, the furniture, papers, everything perfection.

QUEEN VICTORIA, DIARY 1855

BALMORAL

Grampian

QUEEN Victoria and Prince Albert first came to the Balmoral estate in 1842 as guests of Sir Robert Gordon, on the advice of Victoria's Scottish physician Sir James Clark. Both the Queen and the Prince Consort suffered from rheumatism, and it was thought that the climate of upper Deeside might do them some good.

Following Sir Robert's death in 1847, his brother the Earl of Aberdeen suggested that Victoria and Albert might like to take over the lease on Balmoral. There was a problem. Though Victoria was Queen Empress of the greatest empire in history, she had little personal wealth. The money was found to purchase the estate, but plans to rebuild the castle looked in doubt. Then the Queen heard that she had been left £500,000 for her personal use in the will of the eccentric barrister John Camden Neild. She adored Balmoral, as her diary entries show.

Every year my heart becomes more fixed on this dear Paradise, and so much more so now that all has become my dear Albert's own creation, own work, own building, own laying out, as at Osborne; and his great taste and the impress of his clear hand have been stamped everywhere.

QUEEN VICTORIA

Opposite:
BALMORAL CASTLE C1890
B268002

Above:
BALMORAL CASTLE C1890
B268001

THE LOCHS

Had Loch Lomond been in a happier climate, it would have been the boast of wealth and vanity to own one of the little spots which it incloses ...

FROM Glencoe we passed through a pleasant country to the banks of Loch Lomond, and were received at the house of Sir James Colquhoun, who is owner of almost all the thirty islands of the Loch, which we went in a boat next morning to survey. The heaviness of the rain shortened our voyage, but we landed on one island planted with yew, and stocked with deer, and on another containing perhaps not more than half an acre, remarkable for the ruins of an old castle, on which the osprey builds her annual nest. Had Loch Lomond been in a happier climate, it would have been the boast of wealth and vanity to own one of the little spots which it incloses, and to have employed upon it all the arts of embellishment. But as it is, the islets, which court the gazer at a distance, disgust him at his approach, when he finds, instead of soft lawns, and shady thickets, nothing more than uncultivated ruggedness.

SAMUEL JOHNSON, 'A JOURNEY TO THE WESTERN ISLES OF SCOTLAND', 1775

AN excursion steamer waits at the pier on Loch Katrine (above, L93002). The loch, which is ringed with hills, features in Sir Walter Scott's poem 'The Lady of the Lake'.

> *Where, gleaming with the setting sun,*
> *One burnished sheet of living gold,*
> *Loch Katrine lay beneath him rolled,*
> *In all her length far winding lay,*
> *With promontory, creek, and bay,*
> *And islands that, empurpled bright,*
> *Floated amid the livelier light,*
> *And mountains that like giants stand*
> *To sentinel enchanted land.*

Loch Achray (opposite, 44603), a small stretch of water, is sandwiched between Loch Katrine and Loch Vennachar. This picture shows the Trossachs Hotel situated on the northern shore, and the wooded slopes of Sron Armailte.

Loch Lomond (left, 43209) became a popular destination for day trippers from around Clydeside, especially after the opening of the Dumbarton & Balloch Joint Railway. The loch itself was served by steamers of the Loch Lomond Steam Boat Co, whose first ship, the 'Prince of Wales', was built at Port Glasgow in 1858. Tarbet lies at the eastern end of a neck of land that extends from Arrochar on Loch Long.

Opposite below:
LOCH LOMOND,
THE PIER AT TARBET
1899 *43209*

Opposite above:
LOCH KATRINE,
TROSSACHS PIER
C1890 *L93002*

This page:
LOCH ACHRAY
C1899 *44603p*

STIRLING is the last place where there is a bridge over the Forth before the river widens into an estuary (above, 44701). The town and its castle have therefore been fought over on numerous occasions. Dating from about 1400, the bridge was for years one of only a handful of crossing points over the Forth. In 1745, one of the arches was blown up to prevent Prince Charles Edward's forces from entering the town.

One of Scotland's greatest royal fortresses, Stirling Castle was taken by William Wallace in 1297 but was surrendered to Edward I in August 1305 following a siege. The survivors of the garrison, commanded by Sir William Oliphant, were brought before 'Longshanks' (the king) and made to kneel in supplication. It was here that both James II and James V were born and where Mary, Queen of Scots and James VI both lived for a number of years. The Parliament Hall is close to the Inner Court and James VI's Chapel Royal. Following their defeat at the battle of Dunbar, Major General David Leslie and several thousand survivors of his army took shelter in Stirling. The town eventually fell to General Monk in 1651.

STIRLING

Central Scotland

This view of Stirling's Broad Street (left, 44705) looks towards Mar's Wark. Dating from 1570, this uncompleted renaissance building was intended for use by the Earl of Mar who was Regent at the time.

In June 1314, one of the most decisive battles in Scotland's history was fought at Stirling. The armies of Edward II and Robert I met on the flat fields south of the city. Edward was determined to relieve Stirling Castle by mid summer - it was one of the few Scottish castles still controlled by the English. The Scottish forces were smaller, but had the advantage that they were deployed more effectively. Against huge odds they gained a heroic victory, and Edward and the English forces were driven from the field of battle and out of Scotland. However, it was several years later in 1328 that Edward III, King of England, finally accepted Scotland's right to full independence. The battle of Bannockburn, marked in songs and verses down the centuries, proved the end of any English attempts to control the northern British kingdom.

Opposite: STIRLING, THE BRIDGE 1899 *44701*

Left: STIRLING, BROAD STREET 1899 *44705*

Below left: STIRLING CASTLE 1899 *44696*

Below right: STIRLING, OLD PARLIAMENT HOUSE 1899 *44697*

THE BATTLE OF BANNOCKBURN

… WITH wapynys stalwart of stele
They dang upon, with all thair mycht.
Their fayis resawyt wele, Ik hycht,
With swerdis, speris, and with mase
The battaill thair sa feloun was,
And awa rycht spilling of blud,
That on the erd the sloussis stud.
The Scottsmen sa weill thaim bar,
And awa gret slauchter maid thai thar,
And fra sa fele the lyvis rewyt,
That all the feld bludy was lewyt.

'BARBOUR'S BRUCE' C1370

TINTERN ABBEY

Gwent

EXUBERANT and swift, the River Wye is thought by many to be the most beautiful river in our islands. At Tintern it is at its loveliest, winding a sinuous course around the picturesque old abbey ruins.

It is difficult to imagine from this idyllic scene that Tintern was once heavily industrialised. Records of an iron and wire works here go back to the 16th century, and production continued until the late 19th century. The wire was used, among other things, to make brushes for carding in the wool industry. Remains of the works can still be seen in the Anghiddy Valley in the woods behind Tintern, where the river was dammed in several places to make ponds for use in the iron processing.

Wordsworth has celebrated Tintern and the beauties of the Wye in his famous poem, written in July 1798, as he walked back to Bristol. In it he extols the delights of the river and the brooding hills around it, and tells how they had a profound effect on the development of his poetic sensibility.

I began it upon leaving Tintern, and concluded it just as I was entering Bristol in the evening.

Left:
TINTERN, THE VILLAGE
1925 *76881*

Above:
TINTERN ABBEY 1890
27587

Opposite:
TINTERN ABBEY, FROM
THE SOUTH WEST 1893
32468

FIVE years have past; five summers, with the length
Of five long winters! and again I hear
These waters, rolling from their mountain-springs
With a soft inland murmur. – Once again
Do I behold these steep and lofty cliffs,
That on a wild secluded scene impress
Thoughts of more deep seclusion; and connect
The landscape with the quiet of the sky.
The day is come when I again repose
Here, under this dark sycamore, and view
These plots of cottage-ground, these orchard-tufts,
Which at this season, with their unripe fruits,
Are clad in one green hue, and lose themselves
'Mid groves and copses …

             These beauteous forms,
Through a long absence, have not been to me
As is a landscape to a blind man's eye:
But oft, in lonely rooms, and 'mid the din
Of towns and cities, I have owed to them
In hours of weariness, sensations sweet,
Felt in the blood, and felt along the heart …

WILLIAM WORDSWORTH,
'TINTERN ABBEY' 1798

THIS former Cistercian abbey was founded in 1131 by Walter de la Clare. The first brothers of the establishment came directly from Normandy. The remains to be seen today actually date from the abbey's rebuilding in the course of the 13th to the 15th centuries. The abbey's primary occupation was agriculture, and it reached the apogee of its wealth and influence in the 14th century, when it was reckoned the wealthiest abbey in Wales. The Dissolution of the Monasteries in the 1530s brought the inevitable decline and subsequent neglect of its fabric. Lead from the roof was stripped (to be re-used at Raglan and Chepstow castles), and the ivy-clad ruins were later to become a focus for the romantic travellers of the 18th and 19th centuries. The total length of the church is 228ft; the nave has six bays, the choir four, and the transepts three. In Victorian times it was possible to climb the structure and to walk along the top of the principal walls: 'To anyone with a steady head there is not the slightest risk, and the views which this elevated station commands are exceedingly beautiful'. Today, it is likely such an undertaking would be frowned upon by Cadw, the custodians of the abbey and its grounds!

BEFORE the town council renamed it Queen Street, this road was called Crockherbtown, allegedly because the monks of Greyfriars used to grow pots of herbs here. The tramlines are laid, but the horse still rules supreme. The last Cardiff tram ran in 1950. There is a pleasing trio of horse-drawn vehicles here, from the omnibus and the pony and trap to the humble horse and cart making a delivery to Williams & Sons. Edward Philpot was the 'ale taster'. He checked the pubs for watered-down beer. Nicknamed 'Toby', he had to taste many pints at the Glove and Shears – all in the line of duty!

Above: CARDIFF, QUEEN STREET 1893 *32678*

Opposite above: CARDIFF, THE CASTLE, THE SOUTH SIDE C1903 *32670ap*

Opposite centre: CARDIFF, THE DOCKS 1893 *32696*

Opposite right: LLANDAFF, THE CATHEDRAL 1893 *32699*

CARDIFF
South Glamorgan

It is surprising to remember that Cardiff was only designated a capital in the 1950s. Today it is a cosmopolitan city, with fine public buildings like the civic centre in Cathays Park, the University of Wales College and the City Hall.

However, it was the opening of the Glamorgan Canal from Merthyr Tydfil in 1794, and of the West Bute Dock in 1839, and the coming of the railway, that helped to change Cardiff from a seaside village to the largest town in Wales. By 1901 its population had risen to 164,330 and it was the most important coal exporting port in Britain. In the view of the docks (below left, 32696) the steamer in the foreground is the 'Success', a working boat. Shallow-draught paddle steamers were developed specifically for use in the tidal estuaries, where the water level could become very low.

Cardiff boasts one of the best preserved examples of a Norman motte and keep, which can be seen inside the grounds of Cardiff Castle (left, 32670a). The 3rd Marquess of Bute employed the architect William Burgess to redesign Cardiff Castle in 1868. Highly-coloured and gilded walls and ceilings and tiled floors and exotic wood help to make it a romantic Victorian fantasy.

Llandaff Cathedral (below right, 32699), founded by St Teilo in the 6th century, lies in a hollow, sited so as to be shielded from the Vikings.

ST MARY STREET

RHONDDA VALLEY
Mid Glamorgan

THE name Rhondda is one of the most evocative of all. To most people it signifies just two things, coal and male voice choirs.

The Rhondda is a region that consists of two valleys in mid-Glamorgan, each about 16 miles long and never as much as a mile wide. The twin valleys run north to south, and lie approximately fifteen miles north of Cardiff, the Welsh capital. The Rhondda Fawr river (Big Rhondda) runs for ten miles, while the Rhondda Fach (Small Rhondda) is seven miles long. The two valleys form a V shape, and come together in the south of the Rhondda at the confluence of the two rivers in the appropriately named town of Porth, meaning 'gateway'.

In the early 19th century, when the Rhondda was described as 'wild and untameable', there were no roads into the valleys, and indeed why should there have been? It was simply densely forested, abounding with game and wildlife. It was said that a squirrel could travel tree by tree from the river's source at the head of the valleys all the way down to Pontypridd without touching the ground.

All this was to change – and rapidly. Soon after 1860, tentative mining explorations had taken place in the quiet, lush valleys, and black gold was struck – vast deposits of bituminous and steam coal were found. At that time, the two valleys housed around 3,000 people. By 1910, nearly 150,000 were squeezed into the available land, in ranks and terraces of houses grouped around 40 or so pitheads. However, by the 1980s it was all but over for the Welsh coal industry. Though far from exhausted, the Rhondda deep mine pits were considered uneconomic.

It is often assumed that the all but absolute death of the coal industries has left the landscape irreparably scarred, and the people diminished and embittered. But that would be to underestimate the hardy spirit of the valley communities. In fact, the Rhondda is now an area undergoing a remarkable regeneration. Here the beauty has returned, and the mountains are again green; there are no more coal tips and slag heaps, whose great peaks stood like the pyramids of old, reaching up to the sky. Fish can swim again in the clear river Rhondda, which rises at Blaenrhondda and flows through Treherbert and down the valley all the way to Porth and beyond.

Left:
YNYSHIR, THE PIT
C1965 *Y33001a*

Below left:
TONYPANDY,
CLYDACH STREET
C1955 *T192008*

Opposite left:
CWMPARC, PARC PIT
C1955 *C391005*

Opposite above:
TONYPANDY,
GENERAL VIEW
C1960 *T192002*

Opposite below:
YNYSHIR, GENERAL
VIEW C1965 *Y33002*

TONYPANDY'S name is derived from the fulling mill built there in 1738. The rope-worked incline at Pwllyrhebog near Tonypandy was worked by specially-designed engines right up to 1951. The lift at Tonypandy station was unique in that it worked from the up platform to street level, and was hydraulically worked by using water from the nearby river.

The infamous riots at Tonypandy in 1910 were important because of the changes they brought about in early industrial relations - the battle was between the nobility who owned the mines and their workers, from whom they demanded absolute obedience and submissiveness. These men worked 12-hour shifts in the most dangerous conditions for barely a living wage. 12,000 miners went on strike and hundreds of police were sent in to keep order. With the death of a miner the strike became a full-blown riot, and instead of negotiating Winston Churchill sent in the army to quell the unrest. This caused deep, lasting anger.

Cwmparc (below, C391005) had some of the best coal in the Rhondda. As well as the mighty Parc Pit, the Dare Colliery was located here. It was sunk in 1866, and by 1890 was producing 184,000 tons of coal per year from a workforce of 748 men and boys. It finally closed in February 1964.

Ynyshir is an excellent example of a Rhondda pit village (below right, Y33002), and shows how it was necessary to build the terraced houses in a string along the valley bottom. Hemmed in by the mountains, it was the only way they could go; this is the reason why so many towns in the area almost meet. The pit is up the Rhondda Fach valley. The immense winding house and gear dwarfs the tiny cottages behind.

WELSH CASTLES

Pembrokeshire

Pembroke standeth upon an arm of Milford, the wich, a bout a mile beyond the towne, creketh in so that it almost peninsularith the town that standeth on a veri maine rokki ground .

JOHN LELAND 1710

PEMBROKE Castle began its life as a far humbler structure than we enjoy today, once described as '... a slender fortress of stakes and earth'. This view of the castle perhaps best illustrates its superb defensive position. First fortified with a wooden structure in 1093, the castle was the only one in the area not to fall when the Welsh rose against the Normans in 1094. To the left is the Pembroke Corn Mill, a tidal mill, destroyed by fire in the 1950s. The fortifications of the castle once surrounded the entire town to protect it from attack. Pembroke was also an important port and quays can still be seen under its walls. The castle owes its origins to Roger de Montgomery, the Earl of Shrewsbury, who invaded Dyfed shortly after the Conquest in 1093. The vegetation clearly in evidence was removed after Major General Sir Ivor Philipps acquired the castle in 1928. The new owner also undertook some restoration of the 17th-century damage.

PEMBROKSHIRE abounds in imposing old castles, churches and old mansions. With its precipitous coasts, picturesque resort towns, old fishing harbours and exquisite cathedral at St Davids, the county is blessed with a treasure house of antiquities and places of interest.

Carew Castle (right, 27998) was reputedly part of the dowry of Princess Nest, the bride of Gerald of Windsor in 1100. Originally a motte and bailey, it was extensively developed by Sir Nicholas Carew and, after his death in 1311, by his son. In 1480 the castle was leased to a Welsh lord, Rhys ap Thomas, who rebuilt and extended it. He was host to the last great tournament held in Wales – 600 knights feasted and jousted here for five days to celebrate his being made a Knight of the Garter. Today the ivy has been removed, and the buildings have been carefully preserved.

The evocative view of Haverfordwest, from the north-east part of the town below the castle walls, shows the impressive castle and prison (below right, 27940). The watchtower in the roof of the new prison was built so that the guards could observe all activity in the prison exercise yards. These buildings in the shadow of the castle walls were the site of the Marychurch Foundry, the town's biggest employer until its closure in the mid 1930s.

Manorbier's splendid castle (illustration, below) is six miles from Tenby, and has commanding views. It is probably the oldest surviving stonework in the county. It was originally an earth and timber structure begun by Odo de Barri in the 12th century. Giraldus Cambrensis, the famous chronicler, was born here and was obviously very attached to the place: he wrote that it was 'conspicuous for its grand appearance as for the depth of its waters; and a beautiful orchard on the same side inclosed on the one part by a vineyard ... It is evident, therefore, that Maenor Pirr [Manorbier] is the pleasantest spot in Wales.'

MANORBIER CASTLE

Opposite:
PEMBROKE CASTLE 1890
27955

Above:
CAREW CASTLE 1890
27998

Left:
HAVERFORDWEST,
THE CASTLE FROM THE
RIVER 1890 *27940*

HAD it been otherwise, I must long ago have perished; but as it was, it is surprising how easily and securely my little and light boat could ride. Often, as I lay still at the bottom and kept no more than an eye above the gunwale, I would see a big blue summit heaving close above me; yet the coracle would but bounce a little, dance as if on springs, and subside on the other side into the trough as lightly as a bird. I began after a little to grow very bold and sat up to try my skill at paddling. But even a small change in the disposition of the weight will produce violent changes in the behaviour of a coracle.

ROBERT LOUIS STEVENSON, 'TREASURE ISLAND', 1883

CORACLES

Carmarthenshire

CORACLES date back to prehistoric times, the fishermen making their own coracles from a framework of ash laths covered by hides. Pliny, quoting Timaeus, says that 'the island of Mictis [St Michael's Mount in Cornwall], in which the tin is produced, is distant inwards from Britain six days' voyage, and that the Britons sail to it in vessels made of wicker-work covered with hide.'

When Carmarthen was the centre for the woollen trade, flannel was used in the construction of coracles. It was prepared with pitch and tar as a covering for the shell. When flannel was too dear, canvas was used.

At the beginning of the 19th century there were about 400 coracles on the Tywi. The men worked in pairs with a net stretched between the two coracles. When they had fished their short stretch of river they carried their craft on their backs and stored them in their gardens. Now only 12 pairs are allowed.

CENARTH, or Kenarth as it is often spelled, is situated alongside the River Teifi and the Cardiganshire border; here the ancient coracle is still in regular use for the salmon fishing. The men work in pairs a few yards apart, and speedily lift the net at the slightest movement of a salmon.

Coracles are also used at Cenarth for handling sheep during the process of dipping them in the river (above, C376035). The drovers and dogs would drive the sheep into the water, forcing them to swim to the other side and thus get a thoroughly good dipping. They valued their sheep – the coracle men took to the river to ensure they all got across safely.

Opposite:
CARMARTHEN, CORACLES 1898
41093p

Above:
CENARTH, SHEEP DIPPING
C1960 *C376035t*

209

IN translation, Tal-y-Llyn means 'the end of the lake': that aptly describes the location of the village (above, 88048), with its little church and inns in the shadow of Cadair Idris. It sits at the south-western end of the lake, where the River Dysynni comes tumbling out in a series of little cascades. The lake has always been famous for trout fishing. This view of Tal-y-Llyn lake - Llyn Mwyngil in Welsh - looks much the same today, with the slopes of Cadair Idris rising up on the left. On the right-hand shore the B4405 snakes along towards Cross Foxes and Dolgellau.

Corris, which gave its name to the Welsh narrow-gauge railway line (right, 44555), is a slate-quarrying village in the valley of the Afon Dulas. Slates are used here not just for roofing but for numerous other purposes, including fencing. The narrow gauge railway ran from Machynlleth to Corris. It was opened in 1859 and closed, following flooding, in 1948. This locomotive is now used on the Tal-y-Llyn railway.

The famous bridge at Barmouth (below right, 37685) spans the Mawddach estuary. A train is heading south. The railway was built as part of the Cambrian railway, with two stations, Barmouth and Barmouth Junction.

CADAIR IDRIS

Gwynedd

Opposite: TAL-Y-LLYN, THE LAKE 1937 *88048*

Above: MACHYNLLETH, THE CORRIS RAILWAY 1899 *44555*

Below: BARMOUTH, THE RAILWAY BRIDGE 1896 *37685*

[The old man] took me down to a rude 2-roomed hut built of huge stones by his father just under the shelter of the peak, and produced for my benefit a hard-boiled egg and some slices of bread and butter. Also he gave me a woollen comforter to wrap round my neck. Then he vanished. The mist drove in white sheets and shapes past the doorless doorway and past the windows from which the window frames had been removed and the wind whistled through the chinks in the rude walls of huge stones ... It is said that if any one spends a night alone on the top of Cader Idris he will be found in the morning either dead or a madman or a poet gifted with the highest degree of inspiration. Hence Mrs Hemans' fine song 'A Night upon Cader Idris'. The same thing is said of the top of Snowdon and of a great stone at the foot of Snowdon. Old Pugh says the fairies used to dance near the top of the mountain and he knows people who have seen them ... Down, down and out of the cloud into sunshine – a wonderful and dazzling sight. Above and hanging overhead the vast precipices towered and loomed through the clouds, and fast as we went down the mist followed faster and presently all the lovely sunny landscape was shrouded in a white winding sheet of rain ... As we entered Dolgelly the old man said, 'You're a splendid walker, Sir', a compliment which procured him a glass of brandy and water.

THE REVEREND FRANCIS KILVERT 1871

HARLECH

Gwynedd

ALTHOUGH built by Edward I, Harlech is considered the most Welsh of the Edwardian castles. It was here, in the early 14th century, that the rebel leader Owain Glyndwr had his stronghold and seat of power during the rebellion. The massive towers and walls withstood some of the earliest cannon used in Britain, and its starving inhabitants only surrendered after a lengthy siege. The castle was begun in 1283.

The town clusters around the stronghold, clinging to the steep slopes in a series of steeply inclined roads. Harlech Castle is the very image of a medieval stronghold. Imposingly set on its crag overlooking the sands of Morfa Harlech and the famous golf course, it is little changed today from this view. The song 'Men of Harlech' relates to its eight-year siege during the Wars of the Roses.

At Harlech golfers can enjoy the picturesque prospects of the castle and the headland as they walk between holes. The links were created on the Morfa (marsh or sea brink), a tract of well-drained land from which the sea has receded. The greens are well-protected by sand dunes, which in places assume fantastic shapes.

Left:
HARLECH,
THE CASTLE 1889
21737

Below left:
HARLECH,
HIGH STREET 1930
83614

Opposite:
HARLECH,
THE CASTLE AND
THE GOLF LINKS
1908 *60251*

Men of Harlech

March ye men of Harlech bold, Unfurl your banners in the field,
  Be brave as were your sires of old, And like them never yield!
What tho' evry hill and dale Echoes now with war's alarms,
  Celtic hearts can never quail, When Cambria calls to arms.
By each lofty mountain, By each crystal fountain,
  By your homes where those you love Await your glad returning,
Let each thought and action prove True glory can the Cymru move,
  And as each blade gleams in the light, Pray 'God defend the right!'

Clans from Mona wending, Now with Arvon blending,
  Haste with rapid strides along The path that leads to glory,
From Snowdon's hills with harp and song. And Nantlle's vale proceeds a throng,
  Whose ranks with yours shall proudly vie, 'And nobly win or die!'
March ye men of Harlech, go, Lov'd fatherland your duty claims,
  Onward comes the Saxon foe, His footsteps mark'd in flames;
But his march breeds no dismay, Boasting taunts we meet with scorn,
  Craven like their hosts shall flee Like mists before the morn.

ABOUT *twelve miles from Barmouth, Harlech Castle guards the entrance to the estuary of the Traeth. From the line of hills overlooking the level plain a precipitous crag juts forth, its level summit just large enough to support the castle. The view, as may be supposed, is of unusual interest. Immediately below, looking northward, we have the great plain of Morfa Harlech – once a stagnant marsh, the haunt, as it was fancied, of evil spirits, whose baleful fires might be seen glancing hither and thither through the darkness of the night – but now reclaimed; its regular lines of dykes and enclosures making it resemble a piece of green carpet work.*

VICTORIAN GUIDEBOOK

QUARRYING AT BLAENAU

Merioneth

UP at seven o'clock to a gloomy morning ... From the churchyard of Festiniog, at the back of this house, there is the noblest view of black, dreadful mountains to the west, and of the sweet vale of Festiniog to the south, with its river, its bridges and all its charms!

JOHN BYNG 1793

MERIONETH forms the southernmost section of the Snowdonia National Park. The highest mountain groups are the Rhinogs, the Cadair Idris range, the Arennigs and the Arans, but there are also windswept areas of vast upland moors, and numerous lakes. Great rivers, disgorging into three wide estuaries, run from east to west – the Dwyryd, the Mawddach and the Dyfi. These were formidable obstacles to communication in the past, and they divide Merioneth into two distinct blocks. Merioneth has significant mineral resources. Massive slate beds, particularly in the Ffestiniog area in the north, have been heavily exploited, although the geology required that the slate was mined underground, not quarried as in the former Caernarvonshire. There are also metals here, including manganese ores, and, most importantly, gold.

FORMERLY the slate capital of Wales, this slate-grey mountain town is proud of its history and happily promotes its memory. The quarries, which roofed Victorian England from London to Birmingham and back, now offer various tours, and the Ffestiniog narrow-gauge railway carries passengers, rather than slate, to the coast at Porthmadoc. This sunlit view looks across the town towards the great heaps of waste from its slate mines. The railway can be seen on the left.

The Oakley Quarry (right, 46746) was one of Blaenau's major quarries; it closed after the Second World War. Ffestiniog slate is of very high quality, and can be split into very thin sheets of great length. It has to be mined because the slate beds dip under a cover of other rocks. The non-slate rocks form huge tips of waste material that scar the hills around, creating a surreal and fantastic landscape.

The photograph of Church Street (below, 46742) looks uphill towards the great cliff of Carreg Du, which looms over the town's streets. On the right is Owen's butcher's shop, whose hanging meat display would be a health inspector's nightmare. A striped barber's pole projects out over the street, and just beyond is the Temperance Hotel and W J Penny, who sells ales and spirits.

In the photograph of the station at Blaenau Ffestiniog massive waste tips tower above the railway company's offices and the quarrymen's terraced houses. Only about one-tenth of the rock quarried is actually usable for roofing slates. The rest forms these great spoil heaps that are such a feature of the North Wales industrial landscape.

Opposite: BLAENAU FFESTINIOG, GENERAL VIEW 1901 *46735*

Above: BLAENAU FFESTINIOG, CHURCH STREET 1901 *46742*

Above right: BLAENAU FFESTINIOG, OAKLEY QUARRIES 1901 *46746*

Below right: BLAENAU FFESTINIOG, DUFFWS STATION 1901 *46744*

SNOWDON, rising to 3,565 feet, is the highest mountain in Wales. Mountain guides offered their services to intrepid Victorian walkers wanting to ascend Snowdon. The serious expression on the faces of the young men (left, 30162), one clad in plus fours, posing for their photograph on the summit cairn, suggests the effort involved. A number of wooden cabins, euphemistically described as 'hotels', offered shelter and refreshment. They were replaced in 1936.

A GLORIOUS day. Snowdonia magnificent … but the glory was what I never saw before, all those grand mountains, 'silver-veined' with rills, cataracts of snow-white threads, if you will, zigzagging down every rock face – sometimes a thousand feet – and the whole air alive with the roar of waters. The greenness and richness of the mountains after our dusty burnt-up plains, is most refreshing …

I wish I could tell you what colour the mountains are. Not pink, not purple, not brown, but a sort of pale pink madder, with vast downs of bright green grass interspersed.

CHARLES KINGSLEY 1856

SNOWDONIA
Gwynedd

THIS 3,565ft-high mountain is the highest in England and Wales. Its Welsh name is Yr Wyddfa, said to mean 'the great burial place'. Today the mountain gives its name to the Snowdonia National Park, playground for outdoor sports enthusiasts. The area has always been hugely popular, ever since the first recorded ascent of Snowdon in 1639 by Thomas Johnson, a botanist.

Here we see a train nearing the summit at Snowdon. One of the Swiss-built steam locomotives propels the standard single coach up the final leg; the railway starts near the Victoria Hotel, 350ft above sea level, and there are four intermediate stations before the summit is reached. A return trip takes some two hours. Snowdon consists of four rugged and precipitous ridges separated by 100ft-deep hollows, and is formed of slate and porphyry.

Opposite above:
SNOWDON, THE SUMMIT HOTELS AND
THE SUMMIT CAIRN 1892   *30162*

Opposite below:
SNOWDON, THE MOUNTAIN RAILWAY
1896   *37764*

Opposite left:
BEDDGELERT, THE BRIDGE 1889
21832

Left:
SNOWDON, THE MOUNTAIN RAILWAY
1897   *40059p*

ON one occasion [David Cox] was out in a field at Bettws, painting in oils, accompanied by an artist. His companion, hearing him throw his pallet down with a dash, and exclaiming, 'It's no use, I can't do it!' hurried to Cox, and found him about to wipe his picture off the canvas. 'Mr Cox!' he exclaimed, 'what are you doing?' 'Oh,' he replied, 'I can't manage it at all to my satisfaction, and must wipe out my work.' The picture was a very nice one; so after some further remonstrances, Cox said, 'Well, I want a tube of Indian yellow, and if you have one to spare, and will give it me in exchange for my picture, you shall have it.'

QUOTED IN N NEAL SOLLY'S 'LIFE OF DAVID COX' 1873

FOR many years, the painter David Cox (1783–1859) made Snowdonia his headquarters in North Wales. The scenery is unusually varied and beautiful, with the mountains and huge skies, surrounded by rocky glens and deep wooded valleys.

This magnificent view (opposite, 84742) shows Beddgelert cupped in an encircling ring of mountains. It was described in the late 1890s as 'nestling in a deep romantic vale, engirt by lofty mountains, amidst the grandest scenery in Wales'. It is the perfect site for the ancient priory that once stood here; it was attached to the church of St Celert, and pilgrims have made their way here down the centuries.

The famous resort of Betws-y-Coed is on the Holyhead road, in the narrow, deeply-glaciated valley of the river Conwy. It became popular when it was reached by the railway in Victorian times, and has remained a tourist honeypot ever since. There are several fine Victorian hotels from which visitors can still explore the fine landscape and foaming rivers.

The lake of Dyffryn Mymbyr lies in a broad, windswept upland valley. Beside the stone causeway and bridge, rowing boats invite anglers or sightseers to venture out on the water. Capel Curig village stands at the junction of valleys on the London to Holyhead road.

Opposite:
BEDDGELERT,
THE VIEW
TOWARDS
SNOWDON 1931
84742

Above left:
BETWS-Y-COED,
THE RIVER c1876
8580

Below left:
CAPEL CURIG,
THE BRIDGE
c1870 *5100*

CAERNARFON
Caernarfon

KNOWN today for its massive castle, one of Edward I's chain of fortresses built to subdue the Welsh, this town on the shore of the Menai Strait at the mouth of the River Seiont is now staunchly Welsh-speaking. It was formerly an important harbour, shipping a variety of goods. It is an ancient place, originally Segontium, a Roman fortress constructed in AD 78. The massive castle, begun in 1285, remains unchanged since this picture was taken. In contrast, the shipping in the harbour has changed dramatically. Here, schooners, including the 'Catherine' in the foreground, lie alongside the slate quay, waiting to be loaded with Snowdon slate for transportation to Europe.

In the view of the square (above, 85673), people are enjoying the broad open space. The town consists of ten streets within the walls, which are defended by round towers, and about twenty outside. It is the capital of the county, and in the late 1890s held assizes and sessions; it was also the militia headquarters.

Above:
CAERNARFON,
CASTLE SQUARE
1906 *54825*
Opposite:
CAERNARFON,
THE CASTLE 1891
29499

THERE are more dogs in Welsh towns than I ever met with in other places, who are eternally fighting, or kick'd and whip'd about; surely every person must join in a wish for a dog tax, to remove so dangerous a nuisance. JOHN BYNG 1787

The currents and eddies in this part of the Menai Strait can be treacherous. HMS 'Conway' (left, M61118) was a training ship run by the Mercantile Marine Services to train officer cadets. She was moved to the shelter of the Menai Strait in 1941 to avoid air raids. As she was being returned to Birkenhead towed by two tugs, she ran aground near Menai Bridge on 14 April 1955.

This station (L311031, below left) was opened in 1848. Although a medieval hamlet of Pwllgwyngyll (meaning 'the white hazel pool') is recorded in the 13th century, the lengthy version of the village's name only appeared circa 1870 in some doggerel verses written by a Menai Bridge tailor. Welsh costume and unusual place names were eagerly exploited by the tourist industry in Wales, as elsewhere.

From Conway a fine and striking road along the seashore, and round the base of Penmaen More, a mountain nearly as high as Snowdon; crossed the Menai Bridge at dusk, with barely light enough to see the wonderful work … This is a most delightful place on the margin of the Strait with the mountains in full view, presenting as the clouds sweep round and over them, and as they are ever and anon lit up by the sun, glorious combinations and varieties of light and shade.

CHARLES GREVILLE 1841

MENAI
Caernarfon

We are looking from Anglesey to the mainland along Telford's suspension bridge (left, 23187). The bridge was the first structure of its kind in the world, and is pictured here when it was 64 years old.

It was built over the Menai Strait by Thomas Telford in 1826 as part of his Holyhead Road, and gave its name to the little town on the northern side of the narrow strait, between the island of Anglesey and mainland North Wales. High arches with tapering piers support the bridge on either shore. These are 153 feet in height; the suspended part of the bridge is 580 feet long, and around 100 feet above high-water mark. The roadway hangs from 16 chains. The total cost of the bridge was £120,000.

The bridge is best viewed from Belgian Promenade, which overlooks the water. Rip tides up and down the strait made the ferry a dangerous option, and earned the Menai the nickname 'the British Bosphorus'.

Beaumaris is one of Anglesey's best-known sailing resorts, at the eastern end of the Menai Strait (below left, 53029). It was founded by Edward I, who built one of his great castles here, although it was never finished. In this view, two old salts and a boy look out across the pier and the Menai Strait to the mountains of Snowdonia. Beaumaris was popular with tourists: it offered fine bathing grounds, pleasant walks and a ferry to Bangor.

Opposite above:
MENAI, THE WRECK OF HMS 'CONWAY' 1955
M62118

Opposite below:
LLANFAIRPWLL,
THE RAILWAY STATION
C1940 *L311031*

Above:
THE MENAI SUSPENSION BRIDGE 1890 *23187t*

Left:
BEAUMARIS, WEST END 1904
53029

BELFAST

Northern Ireland

THE second largest city in Ireland, just over 100 miles north of Dublin, Belfast is the capital of Northern Ireland. It is a city born of the industrial revolution, with extensive docks, ship building and heavy industry. The centre is based around Donegall Square, including the magnificent City Hall and the Linen Hall library. Other notable buildings include both Protestant and Catholic cathedrals, and the Victorian Queen's University. South of the city are the Botanic Gardens.

Corn Market (below, 40184) reminds us of Belfast the market town; the view looks from Arthur Square. Since the famine and the ending of the restrictive corn laws, grain was largely an import handled by a number of merchants. The curved building was brand-new at the time the photograph was taken. The building at the end of the view is a prosperous department store in the High Street. The row on the right tells of a not-so-distant past: these are clearly old houses left behind, now forming shops and protected by the essential awning.

Left:
BELFAST,
THE 'DYNAMIC'
1897 40230

Below left:
BELFAST, CORN
MARKET 1897
40184

Opposite:
BELFAST, CASTLE
PLACE 1897 40187

THE 'Dynamic' (above, 40230) was one of a fleet of six owned by the Belfast Steamship Company. She was one of its express boats, which provided a nightly service to Liverpool from Donegall Quay. Cargo went from York Dock. Behind can be seen the crammed yard of Harland & Wolff, where the 'Dynamic' had been built 14 years earlier. In 1897 eleven new ships were delivered, including the 'Pennsylvania' for the Hamburg Amerika Line - according to The Belfast Newsletter, the largest in the world. At its height the ship building industry in Belfast employed nearly 9,000 men, who delivered eight sizeable ships during a year.

So profitable was the dock at Belfast that the city burghers built a superb custom house. Here, the masters of ocean-going ships came to report their arrival with goods on which they had to pay duty.

The River Lagan flows within a few miles of the huge Lough Neigh, which is bordered by four Ulster counties; a lot of work was done to make the river able to take barges, with a link to the lough. It was never very profitable, but it carried a considerable amount of traffic. Most of the traffic was coal, which was loaded in the harbour beyond the bridge and taken to the linen mills along the river, but there was also a steady flow of sand downstream to this wharf. The long 21-arch bridge built across the Lagan in the 17th century served the city for a very long time; it was Victorian Belfast which built the present five-arch Queen's Bridge. It had to be widened soon afterwards.

THE horse-drawn trams in Castle Place (above, 40187) were a long-established feature of the city, and at the time of this photograph the system was still being extended up the Cregagh and Anderstown Roads. All parts could be reached from this corner, and its popular name of Castle Junction had become fixed. The 114 cars and 1,000 horses were the property of the Belfast Street Tramway Company. The company was now ready to bring in electric trams, and had an Act of Parliament approving the work. However, this was subject to having the approval of the Corporation, which was not forthcoming. As things stood, the company operated under a lease from the Corporation under which it paid rent for the use of the streets. The Corporation had just gained some experience in supplying electricity for light in the city centre from a station in Chapel Lane. The demand of the trams would make it all the more worthwhile to carry on with plans to build a more substantial power station on East Bridge Street by the river, using imported coal. Without doubt, the councillors' thinking was influenced by their experience of running a gas works at a very good profit. Even then, it was producing the money to build a splendid new City Hall, which was to become the perfect memorial for those years. The company made three offers to the Corporation, including one with profit sharing, but to no avail. With another seven years for the lease to run, the city had to wait until 1905 for the new trams.

GIANT'S CAUSEWAY

County Antrim

THE character of Antrim's coast is nowhere better expressed than where it is possible to see the black basalt overlying the chalk rocks, as here at the Wishing Arch (below, 40421). This was a fanciful name given by the Victorians to this 'basalt honeycomb'. From the 18th century, the Causeway was a significant tourist attraction, and its popularity increased greatly when the Belfast to Portrush railway opened in 1883.

Right: THE VIEW FROM THE GRAND CAUSEWAY 1897 *40423*

Below: THE WISHING ARCH 1897 *40421*

Opposite: THE GIANT'S CAUSEWAY, THE LOOM 1897 *40438*

'That's the Causeway before you', says the guide. *'Which?'* *'That pier which you see jutting out into the bay, right ahead'.* *'Mon Dieu! and have I travelled a hundred and fifty miles to see that!'* WILLIAM MAKEPEACE THACKERAY

THE vast collection of basaltic pillars, termed the Giant's Causeway, is situated in the vicinity of Ballimoney, County of Antrim. The principal, or grand causeway, (there being several less considerable and scattered fragments of a similar nature) consists of an irregular arrangement of many hundred thousands of columns, formed of a dark rock, nearly as hard as marble. The greater part of them are of a pentagon figure, but so closely compacted together, that though the pillars are perfectly distinct, the very water which falls upon them will scarcely penetrate between. There are some of the pillars which have six, seven, and a few have eight sides; a few also have four, but only one has been found with three. Not one will be found to correspond exactly with the other, having sides and angles of the same dimensions; while at the same time, the sum of the angles of any one of them are found to be equal to four right angles – the sides of one corresponding exactly to those of the others which lie next to it, although otherwise differing completely in size and form. Each pillar is formed of several distinct joints, closely articulated into each other, the convex end of the one closely fitting into the concave of the next – sometimes the concavity, sometimes the convexity being uppermost. This is a very singular circumstance. In the entire Causeway it is computed there are from 30,000 to 40,000 pillars, the tallest measuring about thirty-three feet.

THE DUBLIN PENNY JOURNAL 1832

THE traveller no sooner issues from the inn by a back door, which he is informed will lead him straight to the Causeway, than guides pounce upon him, with a dozen rough boatmen who are likewise lying in wait; and a crew of shrill beggar-boys with boxes of spars, ready to tear him and each other to pieces seemingly, and bawl incessantly round him ... I was perfectly helpless ... The water was tossing and tumbling into the mouth of the little cave. I looked, – for the guide would not let me alone till I did, – and saw what might be expected: a black hole some 40 feet high, into which it was no more possible to see than into a mill-stone. 'But where, if you please, is the Causeway?' 'That's the Causeway before you,' says the guide. 'Which?' 'That pier which you see jutting out into the bay, right a-head.' 'Mon Dieu! and have I travelled a hundred and fifty miles to see that!'

WILLIAM MAKEPEACE THACKERAY, 'THE IRISH SKETCH-BOOK', 1845

INDEX

FRITH PRODUCTS & SERVICES

Francis Frith would doubtless be pleased to know that the pioneering publishing venture he started in 1860 still continues today. Over a hundred and forty years later, The Francis Frith Collection continues in the same innovative tradition and is now one of the foremost publishers of vintage photographs in the world. Some of the current activities include:

Interior Decoration

Today Frith's photographs can be seen framed and as giant wall murals in thousands of pubs, restaurants, hotels, banks, retail stores and other public buildings throughout the country. In every case they enhance the unique local atmosphere of the places they depict and provide reminders of gentler days in an increasingly busy and frenetic world.

Genealogy and Family History

As the interest in family history and roots grows world-wide, more and more people are turning to Frith's photographs of Great Britain for images of the towns, villages and streets where their ancestors lived; and, of course, photographs of the churches and chapels where their ancestors were christened, married and buried are an essential part of every genealogy tree and family album.

The Internet

Already ninety thousand Frith photographs can be viewed and purchased on the internet through the Frith websites and a myriad of partner sites.

For more detailed information on Frith companies and products, look at these sites:

www.francisfrith.co.uk
www.francisfrith.com
(for North American visitors)

Product Promotions

Frith products are used by many major companies to promote the sales of their own products or to reinforce their own history and heritage. Frith promotions have been used by Hovis bread, Courage beers, Scots Porage Oats, Colman's mustard, Cadbury's foods, Mellow Birds coffee, Dunhill pipe tobacco, Guinness, and Bulmer's Cider.

Frith Products

All Frith photographs are available Framed or just as Mounted Prints and Posters (size 23 x 16 inches). These may be ordered from the address below. From time to time other products - Address Books, Calendars, Table Mats, etc - are available.

See the complete list of Frith Books at:

www.francisfrith.co.uk

This web site is regularly updated with the latest list of publications from The Francis Frith Collection. If you wish to buy books relating to another part of the country that your local bookshop does not stock, you may purchase on-line.

For further information, trade, or author enquiries please contact us at the address below:
The Francis Frith Collection, Frith's Barn, Teffont, Salisbury, Wiltshire, England SP3 5QP.
Tel: +44 (0)1722 716 376 Fax: +44 (0)1722 716 881 Email: sales@francisfrith.co.uk

See Frith books on the internet at www.francisfrith.co.uk

FREE PRINT OF YOUR CHOICE

Mounted Print
Overall size 14 x 11 inches (355 x 280mm)

CHOOSE A PHOTOGRAPH
FROM THIS BOOK

IMPORTANT!

These special prices are only available if you use this form to order .

You must use the ORIGINAL VOUCHER on this page (no copies permitted).

We can only despatch to one address.

This offer cannot be combined with any other offer.

Send completed Voucher form to:
**The Francis Frith Collection,
Frith's Barn, Teffont, Salisbury,
Wiltshire SP3 5QP**

Choose any Frith photograph in this book.
Simply complete the Voucher opposite and return it with your remittance for £2.25 (to cover postage and handling) and we will print the photograph of your choice in SEPIA (size 11 x 8 inches) and supply it in a cream mount with a burgundy rule line (overall size 14 x 11 inches).

Offer valid for delivery to UK addresses only.

PLUS: Order additional Mounted Prints at HALF PRICE - £7.49 each (normally £14.99)
If you would like to order more Frith prints from this book, possibly as gifts for friends and family, you can buy them at half price (with no additional postage and handling costs).

PLUS: Have your Mounted Prints framed
For an extra £14.95 per print you can have your mounted print(s) framed in an elegant polished wood and gilt moulding, overall size 16 x 13 inches (no additional postage and handling required).

Voucher for **FREE** and Reduced Price Frith Prints

Please do not photocopy this voucher. Only the original is valid, so please fill it in, cut it out and return it to us with your order.

Picture ref no	Page no	Qty	Mounted @ £7.49	Framed + £14.95	Total Cost £
		1	Free of charge*	£	£
			£7.49	£	£
			£7.49	£	£
			£7.49	£	£
			£7.49	£	£
			£7.49	£	£

Please allow 28 days for delivery. Offer available to one UK address only

* Post & handling	£2.25
Total Order Cost	£

Title of this book . . . .

I enclose a cheque/postal order for £ . . . .
made payable to 'The Francis Frith Collection'

OR please debit my Mastercard / Visa / Maestro / Amex card, details below

Card Number

Issue No (Maestro only)   Valid from (Maestro)

Expires   Signature

Name Mr/Mrs/Ms . . . .
Address . . . .
. . . .
. . . .
. . . . Postcode . . . .
Daytime Tel No . . . .
Email . . . .

ISBN 1-84589-115-5   Valid to 31/12/08

Free Print – see overleaf

Can you help us with information about any of the Frith photographs in this book?

We are gradually compiling an historical record for each of the photographs in the Frith archive. It is always fascinating to find out the names of the people shown in the pictures, as well as insights into the shops, buildings and other features depicted.

If you recognize anyone in the photographs in this book, or if you have information not already included in the author's caption, do let us know. We would love to hear from you, and will try to publish it in future books or articles.

Our production team

Frith books are produced by a small dedicated team at offices in the converted Grade II listed 18th-century barn at Teffont near Salisbury, illustrated above. Most have worked with the Frith Collection for many years. All have in common one quality: they have a passion for the Frith Collection.
The team is constantly expanding, but currently includes:

Paul Baron, Jason Buck, John Buck, Ruth Butler, Heather Crisp, David Davies, Louis du Mont, Isobel Hall, Lucy Hart, Julian Hight, Peter Horne, James Kinnear, Karen Kinnear, Tina Leary, Stuart Login, Sue Molloy, Sarah Roberts, Kate Rotondetto, Dean Scource, Eliza Sackett, Terence Sackett, Sandra Sampson, Adrian Sanders, Sandra Sanger, Julia Skinner, David Turner, Miles Smith, Lewis Taylor, Shelley Tolcher, Lorraine Tuck, Miranda Tunnicliffe, and Ricky Williams.